HURRICANE IKE: THE LIFE STORIES OF THE RESIDENTS OF THE BOLIVAR PENINSULA, TEXAS

SEPTEMBER 13, 2008:
THE DAY THAT CHANGED OUR LIVES FOREVER!

Compiled by Sarah Terry Standridge

iUniverse, Inc.
New York Bloomington

HURRICANE IKE: THE LIFE STORIES OF THE RESIDENTS OF THE BOLIVAR PENINSULA, TEXAS SEPTEMBER 13, 2008: THE DAY THAT CHANGED OUR LIVES FOREVER!

iUniverse books may be ordered through booksellers or by contacting:

iUniverse
1663 Liberty Drive
Bloomington, IN 47403
www.iuniverse.com
1-800-Authors (1-800-288-4677)

Because of the dynamic nature of the Internet, any Web addresses or links contained in this book may have changed since publication and may no longer be valid. The views expressed in this work are solely those of the author and do not necessarily reflect the views of the publisher, and the publisher hereby disclaims any responsibility for them.

ISBN: 978-1-4401-9845-8 (pbk)
ISBN: 978-1-4401-9846-5 (ebook)

Printed in the United States of America

iUniverse rev. date: 2/02/10

INTRODUCTION

The residents of The Bolivar Peninsula all know it too well, what it has been like and what we have all gone through. We all have our stories to tell. We are all lucky enough to be able to tell them and pass them on. There are some stories that can never be told. Every one of us lost something. Some of us lost everything. There were some residents of the Bolivar Peninsula who, for whatever reason, stayed behind and tried to ride out the storm. We may never know the actual number.

The remains of Caplen and Gilchrist, TX

This book is dedicated to the Bolivar Peninsula residents whom lost their lives during Hurricane Ike. Their memories, their smile, their individuality and their stories will remain in our hearts forever.

All of us that wrote our stories want to share them and to pass them on. We wish for all to understand the brave individuals of our community, The Bolivar Peninsula. The following stories will give insight as to what we all went through during Hurricane Ike (and the aftermath) in September 2008. This book reveals the strength and vigilance of our residents!

May we never have another Hurricane IKE!!!!

CONTENTS

The History of Hurricane IKE xv

Returning to the Bolivar Peninsula xix

Interesting Ike Facts xxi

Hilda Lopez 3

Jeanne Reedy 14

David and Jane Ewing 25

John Jason Cook 30

Anne Osten Christian and Liz Osten Sanders 34

Will Raney 41

Rusty and Sarah Standridge 44

Gene and Jean Straatmeyer 54

Alan and Kimberly Voigt 68

Robin Huber 71

Louise Melilli 75

Katie Coghlan 77

Katie Coghlan 83

Gordan and Cheryl Small 86

Jack Wingfield 90

Jean Block 93

Trish White 97

Wesley Moore 101

Tessa Tedder 103

Tamella Baker 105

Pamela Goza 109

Norma Jean Hedger 117

Michael Clow 120

Linda Wilson 122

Vickie Lee Cash 124

Randy Mattes 126

Judy and Elmer Hay 128

Judy Hay..129

Jessica Lopez..133

Jason Ortiz..135

Zachary Munsch...136

Paulina Cruz...137

Michael Tovar...138

Nivek Sylvestre..139

The Gulf Coast Hurricane History...140

Post Ike: Bolivar Peninsula, Texas Time Line..141

The Bolivar Peninsula Residents
Who lost their lives In Hurricane IKE

IN MEMORIAM

MARION VIOLET ARRAMBIDE, (age 78, Port Bolivar)
MAGDALENA STRICKLAND, (age 49, Port Bolivar)
SHANE WILLIAMS, (age 33, Port Bolivar)
(Above family - mother, daughter and grandson)

ROSE DELORES BROOKSHIRE, (age 72, Port Bolivar)
CHARLES ALLEN GARRETT, (age 42, Port Bolivar)
(Above family - mother and son)

GAIL L. ETTINGER, (age 58, Gilchrist)
WALTER FISHER, (age 70, Port Bolivar)
JENNIFER McLEMORE, (age 58, Gilchrist)
HERMAN "PEE-WEE" MOSELEY, (age 48, Gilchrist)
LEE ANTHONY STANDRIDGE, (age 23, Crystal Beach)

The Bolivar Peninsula Residents Still Missing
HARRY BINGHAM, (age 61, Crystal Beach)
GLENNIS DUNN, (age 70, Crystal Beach)
SUSAN SHEALY, (age 52, Crystal Beach)
SANDY D. WALTON, (age 54, Gilchrist)

(* These are the names released by the "Laura Recovery Center" as of 9/13/09.)

IN MEMORY OF ALL OF OUR PENINSULA PETS,
LIVESTOCK AND WILDLIFE LOST DURING THE STORM.

HURRICANE IKE

Per the Tropical Weather report, Hurricane IKE began as a tropical wave off of the coast of Africa around August 29, 2008. Its style is known as a "Cape Verde" type hurricane as it tracked south of Cape Verde and slowly developed. A few days later, by September 1, 2008 it had developed into the 9th tropical depression of the Hurricane season and was classified Tropical Storm IKE later in the day. IKE underwent rapid deepening on September 3rd into the morning of the 4th. It turned into a Hurricane on September 3, 2008 at 4:00 P.M. It had achieved category 4 strength on the Saffir-Simpson scale at 140 MPH. Shortly after this, northerly wind shear started to take its toll and weaken it north of the Leeward Islands.

IKE underwent another re-strengthening phase as it moved west southwest into the Turks and Caicos and Southern Bahamas. Grand Turk was in the northern eye wall and Great Inagua, Bahamas received a direct hit. Extensive damage occurred throughout these locations, with preliminary estimates showing 80% of the houses on Grand Turk receiving some damage. IKE continued toward Cuba making landfall on the northeast coast of Cuba. It crossed Cuba and turned more west northwest, barely off of its southern coast. After this, IKE made a second landfall in the western part of the country near where Hurricane Gustav made landfall not long before.

IKE began to strengthen immediately after moving into the southern Gulf of Mexico. The Keys received some flooding, had squally weather and reported an isolated tornado. In a similar fashion to Hurricane Gustav, Hurricane IKE had a very low barometric pressure in the central Gulf of Mexico, but did not strengthen significantly. Dry air on the western side of the hurricane kept it from strengthening until just before landfall.

High storm tides flooded the upper Texas and southwest Louisiana coast twenty four hours ahead of landfall. Storm tides of 10-15 feet were common in these areas. **IKE made landfall on September 13, 2008 at 2:10 A.M. on the Bolivar Peninsula of Galveston County.** Even though IKE was classified as a category 2 hurricane with winds reaching over 110 mph; the combination of wind and the massive water surge, it classified as a Category 4 (Four). The heavy rain continued into the mid part of the U.S. as IKE merged with a cold front. Power was lost to approximately 4,500,000 (4 and ½ million) people at the height of the storm.

Hurricane IKE ravaged the Bolivar Peninsula taking nearly everything in its path. The storm surges and wind reduced the community to mere "rubble." It took over 3,600 homes and severely damaged the remaining that stood standing. Its enormous surge came in much quicker than expected leaving people stranded on the Peninsula, forced to "ride out the storm." The floods rose to at least 18 feet above normal tide. The walls of water washed entire homes into the bay beyond the Peninsula, leaving a "bombed-out" landscape of ruins, debris, mud and sand. It not only destroyed the houses and businesses, but also the very land itself. During the day approaching the storm, rescue workers in helicopters saved over 140 people from the flood waters. Immediately after the storm an enormous search and rescue mission was started for the peninsula.

The Bolivar Peninsula is a 27 mile long barrier island just northwest of Galveston, Texas and it includes the communities of Port Bolivar, Crystal Beach, Caplen, Gilchrist and High Island. It was a permanent home for approximately 3,900 residents and it is a huge tourist destination for thousands of beach and wildlife lovers.

In summary, IKE was a HUGE hurricane. **IKE was 70% larger than the average hurricane.** In the central Gulf of Mexico, winds of tropical storm force or greater extended out 275 miles from the center. IKE's effects not only were felt on the coast, but extended well inland. Wind damage and/or flooding rains followed the path of IKE into the southern Great Lakes, Ohio Valley and into New England. Damages estimates are placed at $18 billion, with an additional $4.4 billion in damage in IKE's post tropical stage, making IKE the 3rd costliest hurricane to hit the U.S.

RETURNING TO
THE BOLIVAR PENINSULA

September 25, 2008

Official Document:
Galveston County Office of Emergency Management

Galveston County is planning the start of "Return Home to Bolivar", a mission designed to allow access to residents, property owners and business owners in the Port Bolivar, Crystal Beach, Caplen and Gilchrist communities.

The focus of this program, which starts Friday, September 26, 2008, is to allow citizens into the Bolivar Peninsula to assess and secure their properties, retrieve belongings and meet with insurance adjusters. No citizen will be allowed to stay on the Peninsula, however you may return daily to complete work and leave each evening.

Citizens will have access to the Peninsula via High Island during the hours of 6:00 A.M. - 4:00 P.M. Westbound traffic onto the Peninsula will not be permitted after 2:00 P.M. Law Enforcement Officers will begin vacate procedures from the Peninsula at 4:00 P.M. The bridge over Rollover Pass along Highway 87 has been damaged and has only one lane open to passenger vehicles no wider than 12 feet. Access via the Bolivar Ferry is not available to the general public due to unsafe conditions at the landings in Port Bolivar.

Persons will be stopped at a check point in High Island. You will be required to show proof of identification and residency. A main staging area at the High Island School will be available to distribute ice, water, mosquito spray and hand sanitizer. Also at the staging area, there will be a first aid station to administer tetanus shots and a critical incident stress management team. Mini-staging areas will be located in Crystal Beach at Crenshaw Elementary and the Joe Faggard Community Center with ice and water only. Porta-Cans will be available at all staging areas.

CITIZENS NEED TO BE AWARE OF SEVERAL IMPORTANT POINTS:

- THERE ARE NO EMERGENCY MEDICAL SERVICES OR FIRE/RESCUE SERVICES. THERE IS NO WATER, SEWER, ELECTRICITY OR TELEPHONE SERVICE. (CELLULAR PHONE SERVICE IS LIMITED)

-BE PREPARED TO WALK DISTANCES UP TO ½ MILE. NEIGHBORHOOD STREETS THAT REMAIN, STILL CONTAIN DEBRIS AND MAY BE IMPASSABLE BY VEHICLE.

-DO NOT ATTEMPT TO TAKE ITEMS FROM ANOTHER PERSON'S PROPERTY, THAT IS CONSIDERED LOOTING AND WILL MAKE YOU SUBJECT TO ARREST.

-THERE ARE COUNTLESS SNAKES, ALLIGATORS AND OTHER WILDLIFE RISKS IN THE AREA. USE CAUTION WHEN MOVING OR LIFTING ITEMS.

-HEALTH HAZARDS INCLUDE MOLD, MOSQUITOES AND OPEN SEPTIC TANKS AND SEWAGE. PROTECT YOURSELF FROM THESE TYPES OF RISKS.

-NAILS, BROKEN GLASS, LUMBER AND OTHER HAZARDS AROUND. USE CAUTION SO YOU DO NOT INJURE YOURSELF. ALSO PREPARE FOR THE POSSIBILITY OF FLAT TIRES BY HAVING SPARE TIRES OR FIX-A-FLAT IN YOUR VEHICLE.

-YOU MAY NEED TO USE A LADDER TO ACCESS HIGH-RAISED RESIDENCES. USE CAUTION AS AREAS YOU ARE ACCESSING MAY HAVE SUSTAINED DAMAGE, CAUSING FLOORS AND PORCHES TO COLLAPSE. BE SURE TO BRING SUPPLIES, TOOLS AND EQUIPMENT TO ACCESS AND SECURE YOUR PROPERTY.

PLAN YOUR DAY SO YOU WILL BE PREPARED TO LEAVE THE PENINSULA BY 4:00 P.M. EACH DAY.

(*Letter from the Galveston County Emergency Management)

INTERESTING IKE FACTS

* Galveston County spent $600,000.00 (600 thousand) spraying for mosquito's right after IKE.

* There was 21,000,000 (21 million) cubic yards of debris removed from the Peninsula.

* IKE was the THIRD most expensive disaster in FEMA history, $18 billion (+) in damage.

* It invoked the largest evacuation of Texans in our state's history.

* It was the largest search and rescue operation in history.

* Over 6 million homes lost power in the United States resulting from IKE.

* Maximum Storm Surge - Approximately 15 - 20 feet in Bolivar Peninsula, Texas.

* IKE was a hurricane for 9 days and 21 hours. It was first named a hurricane on September 3, 2008 at 4:00 P.M. C.T.

* At its largest, IKE's tropical storm force winds stretched for 510 miles and hurricane force winds extended 220 miles. Weather radar from Galveston, Texas to Key West, Florida could see its outer bands. **That's 70% larger than an average hurricane.**

* Cincinnati, Ohio even felt winds of 61 mph from Hurricane IKE.

Bal merely left posts of houses once standing

The only remains of a neighborhood block.

HURRICANE IKE:

THE LIFE STORIES OF THE RESIDENTS OF THE BOLIVAR PENINSULA, TX

HILDA LOPEZ

"The Linn House"

As a child, I was not a fan of the beach. Once a year my mother, her sister, and their combined gaggle of kids would head for our yearly trip to the beach. I never could understand why my siblings and cousins were so excited. I was going to have to trade my cool creeks for a salt water gulf, my soft rolling hills for a barren sandy wasteland. By high school the beach had gotten a little better. After all, your chances for a summer romance and a good tan outweighed all the negatives. By college it was the place to be! Heading down to the beach was definitely heading for a party.

I introduced my children to the piney woods of my youth. They loved it. Each weekend we headed for our house on the river. I was content, the kids were happy. Johnny was raised in Port Arthur. Salt ran through his veins. We started going to the river house in the spring and fall and during the summer months we were off to the beach. My kids betrayed me. They replaced their love of the piney woods with a new love. I was out voted, 3 to 1. Dump the river house and buy a beach house. I had lost the battle but not the war. Since I was the one that had to compromise, I got to choose our beach house. It had to be small new house sitting on a small lot and it had to be beach front. The search began. We agreed we would take out time and find a manageable house. A few months later Johnny told me he had bought us a beach house, the "Linn house!" He knew I had requested new, small, no land, but it was beach front. Johnny said one out of four isn't bad.

Like my love for Johnny, my love for the Linn house did not come on a bolt of lightning knocking me off my feet. Slowly it came to be me. It seeped into my pours. It consumed me. Crossing over the intercostals made troubles go away; peace came. Now the house is gone and our beloved peninsula is destroyed.

THE HISTORY

Eighty four years ago the new school at Caplen was lifted by a storm and set in East Bay. Galveston County abandons the school. The Oxford family brought the school back and made it their beach cottage. In 1929, Guy Linn bought the house and it remained in the Linn family for the next 48 years. For the last 33 years it has had our name on the deed but it will always be the Linn house. The true history of the grand old lady was not the physical house but rather was what the house represented. Hospitality… Fun… Love… Family… Friends… And maybe a little cold beer.

THE PENINSULA

The people made the peninsula like no other place that I know of. One of my first experiences in dealing with "the locals" was the building of the deck. I hired a local for a set fee plus cost of materials. When it came time to pay I found out he had charged the materials to me. Before I paid him I went to check and see what he had charged. I got to the lumber yard and they could not find an account in my name or Johnny's name. We even tried Linn since that was the name on the roof of the house. No luck. I ask them to try once more, giving the full name, Dr. John Joseph Lopez. No luck. Then they ask what kind of doctor he was and when I replied a dentist, they knew where they had put the charges. An account had been open to "The dentist on the beach."

We decided that we needed a telephone. I called Southwestern Bell. After answering a long series of questions, I was told they didn't know if they serviced my area but they would research it and call back. Knowing that Claud's Hardware had a phone I called Claud and asked how he got service. He told me to call the Cameron telephone company. The only question I was asked was where I wanted the bill sent. They gave me a number in High Island and told me the next time I headed for the beach to just call this number and I could get my phone installed. Sure, I thought, this is really going to work. I headed for the beach the next Saturday and called. By the time I got to the house the phone was being installed. Billy, the phone man, came in, had a beer and told us the best place to go crabbing.

I interviewed a handyman about some work that I needed done. When I got through he told me, "Well lady if I wanted to work that hard I would move to Beaumont. All I need is enough money to keep me in shrimp and beer."

Then the electrician that showed up a day late. His excuse, "I'd been bar-b-quing since early morning and by the time you called at noon I was so drunk that my breath alone would set the house on fire."

The list goes on and on. The ferry captain that let my first grade grandson drive the ferry from Galveston to Bolivar. The lady, at the cut, that spent days and days teaching my son and his friends all about fishing. The septic tank guy that drives a truck with a large lettered sign on it, which reads, "I really know my shit." The constable that told my children, if any of those Galveston Sheriffs ever give you any trouble just tell them to call your Uncle Joe.

Once Johnny realized that our kids had never seen a beach with blue water and white sand. He took the family to an island. On about the second day of our trip, my son asks if the people here knew about Bolivar Peninsula. When we told him no; he informed us that he was not surprised because if they knew about Bolivar they surely would not be here. After all, he couldn't find one light bulb on the beach.

Yes our water was brown, tar was on the beach, sticker burrs in the grass, days and even nights were hot, jelly fish in the water, but we loved it. "We only needed enough to keep us in beer and shrimp."

CAPLEN

The oldest houses on the beach were in Caplen. They were large. Land went from highway to beach. Families had owned the same houses for generations. In the beginning, families had spent the entire summer at the beach. In the spring, people were sent down to plant gardens. At the beginning of the summer, cows and chickens were sent down by train. No road lead to Caplen. At High Island, one got on the beach and drove to their houses. By the 1950's, each house had been updated to include indoor bathrooms, running water, (now they even had hot water), and some had been as bold as to replace the screens with windows.

When we bought the Linn house, we were the new kids on the block...we were strangers. We only had one thing in common with our neighbors. We, like them, were Catholic. We began updating the house. Twenty-six gallons of white paint brightened the inside, new fabric covered the furniture. Our kitchen now included new cabinets, a stove with all the burners working, and even a dishwasher. A sun deck was added. Our neighbors where not impressed. They came. They looked. They nodded. They smiled. Each and everyone had the same comment. "I'm glad you kept the hanging beds." But one could tell they thought these new kids were going to ruin the neighborhood.

Going west from the Linn house our nearest neighbor was the Holland family. Not only did fresh air come in from all sides of the house but also from the hole in the floor. When electricity came to the beach, they placed their hot water heater inside of an old fireplace. After all, they didn't use the fireplace anymore. Their son's small sail boat was stored on one of the beds. The next house belonged to the Ball family. And what a house it was. Originally built by a ship captain the same way a ship is built. Sadly, that masterpiece burned sometime in the late 80's. The next two houses belonged to the church. The Bishop's house was a retreat for area priests. It had once belonged to the Brown family. The next house was the nun's house. One could always tell if a nun was walking the beach. They walked the beach in pairs, with their stark white legs and their folded hands.

Directly east of our house was a vacant lot and then the Broussard house. This house was nearly a mirror image of our house. The house was only in use two or at the most three weeks in the summer. Then, the Hebert house came. It was now owned by one of the daughters, Mrs. Donovan. Late in the afternoon, Mrs. Donovan's sitter would help her down to the beach. Mrs. Donovan would get into the water swim out past the breakers, head west, swim for at least 500 feet, turn, and swim back to her property. The sitter would help her get out of the water and help her get back into the house. Next was the Green house. We were sure that all the Greens had webbed feet. Early in the morning, the whole flock would be fishing. After the fish quit biting, they along with their labs would start swimming. By night, they would sit around a driftwood fire. No matter how many people they had stuffed into their house visiting, they would still invite our family to stay for dinner. Their wine was good; their beer was cold. The last house in our little community was the Polk house. It was the second oldest house on the beach. Originally it was the Polk ranch house. Years later when Semi Polk sold the house he told Johnny that he sold it to a lady from Galveston who wanted it for her girls. We questioned from Galveston and for her girls? After then, we only called it the whore house.

We learned from our neighbors. It was not the bright wall and new fabrics that made our houses so special. It was the love of the old. It was the memories of the good times. It was family. It was sharing with friends. Years later, the outside of our house needed painting. I searched and searched for the right shade of blue. At one store, I was shown the most horrid shade of blue ever. It had been mixed by mistake. They would sell it to me for four dollars a gallon. And somehow that loud neon blue was just right for the beach house. After all this was Caplen and we knew what really counted.

THE HOUSE

The insurance adjuster wants me to make a diagram of the house with approximate room dimensions. A floor plan is not what we lost. How can one explain that we measure rooms not in feet but how many we can sleep? It seems they do not care that the walls were 12 inch heart of pine, the floor were oak and cypress, the ceilings were high. It was built to catch the wind from every direction.

The insurance also wants to list contents with age and cost of each item. Age and cost has nothing to do with the loss. How does one replace and old, round, leaning oak table that has a heart and a history? Do they not care that we kept repairing it year after year with no thoughts of ever giving it up? We have set around the table and played hundreds maybe even thousands games of cards. Our family and our friends came into the house and sat at the table. Chairs are filled. More chairs are brought in. Floor space is taken. People sat on kitchen cabinet tops. Drinks, food, good times are shared. For years I have set around that table with friends and the friendship has turned into a sisterhood. We even trade stories about the table itself. Yes, it's true that many years ago someone was shot and killed at this very table. Well no, it's not the only shooting at the table but it was the only death. It was a big house, a really big house. We had five sofa's but everyone sat around the little kitchen table.

Everyone sits and talks around the kitchen table but we eat at the picnic table. It came with the house. It was probably made on-site, along with benches on each side. They were strong and very sturdy. To me, this table will always be remembered for the Saturday night seafood dinner. First one covers the table with layers and layers of newspaper and garbage sacks at each end. Fried fish, cold boiled shrimp and crab claws, bar-b-qued crabs, (of course using the Lopez family secret recipe), potatoes, and corn on the cob are piled in the middle. One eats until their paper plate is filled with shells. Then one rolls up a layer of paper and throws it into the garbage sack, grabs another plate and continues with the feast. Years ago, the seat of choice was next to Matt Hall. Matt loved to pick the meat from crab claws but did not like to eat crab. A little taste of heaven was just a fork reach away. Coming in a close second or maybe even a tie is Saturday night gumbo. Too many cooks tasting and adding to the simmering pot only made it better. For years, I made the gumbo but lately I've been known to turn over my cast iron skillet to Wade. The one thing that was always true about the gumbo, each time everyone said that pot of gumbo was the best ever. How does one put a price on an old gumbo pot that has a stain line that shows one where to add water if one is feeding 24 people? The table would only host good food…lots of good food. It would have been a crime against nature to go a season without gallons and gallons of chicken salad, Sandy eggs, lemon squares, chocolate sauce and the world famous chocolate chip cookies. This table pushed against the wall became a stage for our yearly performance of the "boogie down after dinner show" performed by my kids and their friends. On rainy afternoons, we could cover it with sheets and under the table became a secret club house. After two days of rain a friend, not to be named, would tell the kids a storm was coming and they had better crawl under the table to be safe. Three mothers, six plus kids, makes one do anything to get some peace and quiet.

I can put a cost on 10 single beds and 1 queen but what about the hanging beds? Two double beds with sagging mattresses set on iron frames, hanging from chains. They were placed on the south east and the south west corners of the house. There was always a breeze on one or the other. First ones in the house called dubs on those beds. Each could sleep two but has been known to sleep at least four kids. It was a great place for an afternoon nap, rocking a baby, sharing secrets with a friend, or seeing how high one could swing the bed without breaking a window.

The adjuster might question why one would have over 60 windows and 13 ceiling fans. He wouldn't know that air-conditioning is a new thing to Caplen. Before air-conditioning; windows were always up with sticks propping most of them up, ceiling fans were on with a few floor fans for extra wind. The windows were old and leaky. When the wind blew strong and seeped through the windows, the house sang its own song. This wind song filled the house. At night one, would be lulled to sleep with the sound of the surf and morning would be announced with the raising of the sun and the cry of the gull. At night when the rains came, everyone would jump out of bed and run to shut the windows, mop up the wet floors and raid the kitchen for pots to put under the leaks. Then it all changed. A grandson was born; his name is Carter, and he was the perfect child. Johnny saw a bead of sweat on Carter's brow. No longer did I have my perfect house. Roofs were ripped off and replaced with a new non leaking roof. No more wind song. Windows were replaced with new insulated glass. No more wonderful old unfinished porch ceiling. Insulation was added and a new ceiling. Air-conditioning was installed. I learned to love the comfort of the air but always missed the sound and smells it took from me.

A DAY AT THE BEACH

The days at the beach were all the same but yet they were different. When the children, were young the kids and I nearly lived at the beach. The shortest time we stayed was two weeks out of every month and the longest was forty days. Johnny would come on the weekends and two or three of the week nights. Most weeks we had friends and their children join us for the week with their husbands coming on the weekend. The morning began with breakfast. It was usually cold cereal for the kids and a hidden stash of bear claws for the women. Then it was time for the morning swim. The kids playing in the water and the mothers watched from our beach chairs; talking, sunning and watching. Every few minutes a mother would jump up and start slapping her knees. This was the sign to only go knee deep. As the kids grew, the signals changed. Jumping up and slapping one's arm pits became the signal of the day. After morning swim, it was time for lunch. Sand toys and chairs were carried back to the house. The older girls were allowed to go upstairs and take a shower and sneak a coke but the little boys were stripped of their suits and were given an outdoor shower. One mother would rush upstairs and begin making the peanut butter and jelly sandwiches and pouring watered down Kool-Aid. After lunch, the kids were sent to their bed for an afternoon rest. The mothers would shower and then sit down for a cool quiet lunch. Hopefully, it would be chicken salad stuffed in a fresh home grown tomato served with iced sun tea. After we were sure that the kids were asleep or at least in a stupor, the mothers would pull out a dessert that was "too good to share with kids." After lunch, the mothers would lay down to read. It didn't matter if one was reading a great book or a magazine that the pages had yellowed with age. A few words read or at most a page then one drifted off to sleep. As the kids began to wake one by one, they knew the cardinal rule. Be quite! If a mother was woken, it was back to bed for them. Quiet games were played. And, no, Spoons was not a quiet game. They might go under the house to play in the shade and coolness, being careful not to slam the door as they left. After the mothers awoke, it was time for wheels and motors. Go carts, three wheelers, motorcycles, tractors and even cars, (either a dune buggy or the family station wagon), where driven up the drive and around the house. Our kids were early drivers. Any mother could be talked into a driving lesson. Why sit in hot house when one could be in an air-conditioned car. Later on when the sun was not as hot, we would have snacks and all go for an afternoon swim. Sometimes we cut our afternoon swim short. Piled all the kids and mothers into one car and down to west beach we went to watch the Mexicans pull in their long nets or go to the flats and look for olives. This was followed by supper and then all headed for the deck for star gazing and story sharing. By nine the kids headed for bed, with one last reminder---what ever time you wake the mothers up in the a.m. that is time you have to go to bed in the p.m. Then it was mother time. We would congregate back to the kitchen table. Unscrew the cap from the gallon of wine, talk, play cards and solve the world problems.

During the week, our schedule varied very little. We did go crabbing, fishing, built sand castles, work with sand casting. We collected shells, shark teeth and sea glass and other treasures from the beach. These treasures would be carried up under the house and used for the most wonderful things. Only a kid could take some old boards, driftwood, a tar covered hard hat, a couple of plastic bottles and a few light bulbs and build one of the wonders of the world.

On the weekend things changed. Men arrived, grown men, hairy men. Rules changed. The house became louder. Food got better. Beer was introduced and the mothers started drinking earlier. Bedtimes was changed. One could stay up later, swim deeper, drive faster, and even go out in the heat of the day.

As the kids grew so did their number of friends they brought to the house. I always thought 16 people were the limit to sleep. Little did I know that I would see the number double? By the time they were in high school Caplen was no longer hip enough for them. The girls no longer took a morning swim. They spent their time fluffing, curling, and combing their hair. They had to go west to visit friends and to see and to be seen. I was betrayed once again. My kids were even as bold to suggest we sell our house and buy one on the newer part of the beach. I spent less time watching over children but much more time in the kitchen.

College years were yet another change in the beach. Johnny and I would head for the beach on the weekends. He began taking off on Friday so we could have three days at the beach. Life became slower. We slept late. We enjoyed a swim without kids on our backs. We could eat out. We even introduced a colored TV to the house. We enjoyed adult friends that came for a visit. We reintroduced ourselves. We were no longer just Mother and Daddy. We were young lovers again. Three or four times a year the kids would return with their friends. Sleep all morning. Eat a big breakfast. Go west down the beach. Come back sunburned and seldom sober. Eat. Shower. Eat. Off to the bars. By 3 A.M. (bars closed at 2 A.M.) I could quit pacing and be rest assured they all had made it back safely. They would eat again. Then off to bed.

As young college graduates they continued coming to the beach. But this was different. They actually included Johnny and me in their conversations.

They requested favorite foods of their childhood. They brought back out the games and the puzzles. We would divide into teams, Johnny and I on one team and all the young adults of another team. It was trivial pursuit time. Johnny and I would always win and then they threw in the sinker. Who ever heard of an 80's, 90's trivial game? And who cares about which rock band did what?

The biggest change was the introduction of grandchildren. Our children became the rule makers, the bedtime enforcers, the knee slappers. Johnny and I became the rule breakers, the spoilers.

THE END

All is gone now. IKE took our house, the swinging beds, the picnic table and the oak kitchen table. The gumbo pot is gone. Walls of pictures are no more. IKE was able to rob us of what we cherished, even Johnny's Speedo, but IKE was not able to wash away our memories and when one recalls a memory one still has the beach house. We did not lose a house; we lost a way of life.

Let's all sing We Welcome You to Caplen Beach one more time.

We welcome you to Caplen Beach.
Mighty glad you're here.
Come on up and cool your buns
And have an ice cold beer.
It's only been 100 and 5
And at night the mosquitoes eat you alive.
Kids, and cats and dogs are all here.
And we welcome you to Caplen beach.
(Pause)
Unpack the car yourself boy.

And just think as a child I hated the beach.

(This song was written in June, 1977 by Kay, Patty and Hilda)

Charlie-built cross entering Highway 87 onto the Peninsula.

Photo taken by Janet Louise Davis.

JEANNE REEDY

"Coastal People are Survivors!"

It was a calm September day, September 11, 2008 and I was thinking of my friend Michelle Robotham that died in the World Trade Center on 9/11 in 2001. I always lit a candle and placed it by the picture of her that was taken at the beach. I did not light the candle today as I was packing up items and important papers in preparation for the storm, Hurricane IKE that was supposed to be heading for the Texas, Mexico borders.

Some good friends in Houston, Nanci and Rick Koester told us to come to their house to get away from the coast. We were planning on going there, but a long time friend, Sandy Walton, who evacuated with us during Hurricane Rita, said that she was going to stay at the Rancho Carribe Golf Course, where she worked. She needed to take care of the cat that lived there. Sandy loved animals and always adopted strays or unwanted animals. She also had a rat terrier named Ladybug and a cat named Tigger-Too.

I couldn't take all the animals plus our own cat to the house in Houston, so I told Sandy that Bill and I would stay at the beach with her and the pets. We were going to stay in a big beach house in Caplen Shores that I managed. The house slept 28 people, had storm shutters and a large generator that would maintain most of the electricity for the house. We stayed there for Hurricane Gustav a few weeks earlier.

We arrived at the Caplen house on Thursday afternoon. We were really prepared as far as food and supplies were concerned. We had plenty of food, water, clothes, important papers, etc. After we unpacked all our things, Sandy and I started washing all the linens and even cleaned the upstairs bunk room, the other bedrooms and made all 14 beds. I even baked some chocolate chip cookies. We closed all the shutters and nestled in for a good night sleep.

Sandy and Bill awoke about 4 A.M. and Sandy made Bill breakfast. I was still asleep and awoke about 7 A.M. Bill and Sandy were outside on the front deck overlooking the Gulf watching the storm come in. The steps that were about 50 feet from the deck and that went down to the beach had already been taken away by the storm. We stayed out there for about an hour and I started making phone calls to the owner of the house and taking pictures of the current damages.

The house to the left of us facing the Gulf had already lost about 20 feet of dunes. It was a new house. The house to the right of us had already lost its steps going down to the beach. About a half hour later his walkover split in half and floated off to the West. The other house to the right had a hot tub, that was not completely installed and we watched it float out into the Gulf. I called the owner of the house to our immediate right and told him about the current damages and told him that he might lose his hot tub as the storm was eating away at his property at a quick rate.

The water was creating a path to the right and left of us and started to bring in a lot of debris. There was a vacant lot to the left and it was a lower lying area and a lot of debris was coming on shore. The dunes in front of the house we were in had a clay base and appeared to be holding much better. We still felt very safe. Just out of curiosity though, I called Bob Anderson, a good friend who built the house where we were staying and asked him how deep the pilings were. He told me that they were 8 feet deep and all secured to the concrete slab that was under the house. He was in the area and was trying to get off the Peninsula. He told me it was flooded in Gilchrist and he was not able to get out. I told him to stop by the house, so in about 15 minutes he drove into the yard.

We opened a beer and he told me that we needed to get our vehicles out of there because the water may flood them. We left the house with all the vehicles and headed towards Crystal Beach. As we got closer to Crystal Beach the water on the roads was quickly getting deeper. We got to the new strip center that Bob also built and Sandy Walton parked her car there as her car was much lower to the ground than the rest of our vehicles. She parked it in front of the new liquor store. We ran into another good friend Kenny Lane who had parked his vehicle at the Catholic Church in Crystal Beach.

Kenny followed us to the new Galveston County Sheriffs building in Crystal Beach, which was built on an elevated piece of property. Bill and I left our vehicles parked there, thinking it would be pretty safe. Kenny's girlfriend Paula was working at the Ship's Wheel. They were operating by generator. So we went in and had a cold beer. We left there when they decided to close. Kenny offered to take us back to our vehicles and we decided to head for the Golf Course with Sandy. We went about a half a mile and the water was dangerously deep. We couldn't make it to the golf course because of the deep water. We were stuck. Sandy called my cell phone and left a message saying she was stuck like "a Chuck." I did not get the message until Tuesday, as my cell phone was already dead.

The owner of the Ship's Wheel, Pat Murphy, was pulling into his driveway, next to the furniture store in Crystal Beach. So Kenny, Paula, Bill and I went to Murphy's house to ride out the storm. We were sitting in front of his house watching the water rise and the wind started up a little. It was knocking pecans off the trees and they were hitting us in the head. We didn't have any hard hats, so we decided to go into the house.

We had 3 flash lights and a couple of candles. Everyone was worn out, cold and wet, so we decided to go to bed. Bill was already asleep on the couch. I think everyone was in a deep sleep when Kenny woke up to flashing lights and horn honking. He said, "Who was that crazy fool out in the yard?" We were the crazy fools! Kenny looked out the window and Murphy's mom's car and Paula's car were under water and it was the noise coming from the alarm systems. Bill came into the bedroom where I was sleeping and said, "Get up, the water is coming into the house"

I jumped out of bed and the carpet was already ankle deep. Then, I was a little scared. Murphy had just built an office upstairs which was not totally complete. We opened the kitchen door and water came pouring in. We had to go down 2 steps through the garage level to get to the stairs to the upper level. The water was almost waist high. Bill helped me get to the steps because the area had all kinds of items floating around in the room and other items on the floor. I started up the steps and Bill went back to see if he could help Paula get her two dogs, Murphy's two cats and the baby kittens to the upstairs level. Finally, we all made it up the stairs, trying to find something to dry off with in the dark. We found a couple of towels, but we were all cold and wet.

Once we were all up there, we kept watching the water rise up the lower steps, then to the landing. It soon started up the higher steps and we had about 3 steps more before it would enter the room where we were sheltered. Kenny found an attic entrance and checked it out just in case we would have to get to the roof. All we found was a ball-peen hammer to break through the roofing.

We looked around for a radio and found one, but had no batteries for it. Kenny started to build us a raft. We found several coolers and water jugs and Kenny tied them all together with 12-2 electrical wire, as there was no rope handy. I told them I was not going into that water. We sat at the open windows with our heads looking out at the huge amount of debris that was floating by us. First we saw washers, dryers, stoves and refrigerators floating by. Then the items started getting a little bigger. We saw walls, roofs, and finally whole houses going past. Not so funny, one of them had a light in it. I feared I would see someone standing at the window waving their arms crying out, "Help Me". We all knew it was a battery operated light; of course but it was still spooky.

Kenny finally found another radio with 2 "C" batteries. He took the "D" batteries out of one of the flash lights and taped them together with Scotch tape and took a paper clip and taped it all to the battery compartment of the radio. "Voila" we had communication with the outside world. The radio station reported that the eye of the storm was about 10 minutes until landfall over us. The water was staying at this same level, which was about 15 feet deep.

The moon was full so we could see outside, even though it was about 2 A.M. We never felt high winds shaking the house such as our house in Gilchrist used to do when we had high winds. This was a solid brick house although; the new upstairs addition was not brick. At one time the water was about 3 feet from coming into the window.

We heard some loud bangs coming from the downstairs but we could not tell what it was causing the sounds. We thought something had hit the house and we hoped it did not damage the east wall made of brick. We didn't need the structure below us to break apart. Happily, by the next morning the water had receded enough that we could go downstairs. The loud bangs were caused by the 54" flat screen television as it fell over, then the other one was the refrigerator falling over on its face. We could not get it tipped upright, knowing it was full of good food. However, we found another freezer that contained some Popsicles in it and they were still frozen. That is all we had to eat or drink other than some crackers and stale chips Kenny had found. I think Kenny ate some ravioli's too.

After the eye of the storm went over us, the water started to recede. It did not go down very fast, but when it got to the lower landing we knew we were safe and the worst was over. We all felt a little easier and said "Well, we made it through Hurricane IKE on Murphy's Island." We talked about making T-shirts for the 5 of us with that saying on them.

We also gave Kenny a nickname. His new name is "MacGyver" as he was very inventive concerning our safety. We all thanked God for watching over us and thanks for that television show called MacGyver. I did do a lot of praying that night and I thanked God for watching over us.

We sat all day on Saturday watching the water go down. When the water was waist deep Kenny, Paula and Murphy walked out to the highway to go to the Ships Wheel to check out the damages to Murphy's and Millie's bar, the Ship's Wheel. It was destroyed along with the house. He also lost his truck and mother's vehicle. I know it was devastating to him. Little did we know it was just the first of the devastation we would see!

While they were on their walk, an Army helicopter came down on the highway so they could make a potty stop. They said they had been in the air for several hours. They asked the guys if they wanted to be rescued. They said "No, the storm is over" The helicopter personnel gave them a 12 pack of water and 6 MRE's. I think it stands for "meals ready to eat." We heated up the meals and ate. The cookies were good, not saying much for the bread. I ate a Sloppy-Joe MRE. We got a package of matches in each of the kits. We only had one working cigarette lighter and one pack of wet cigarettes that we laid on the desk to dry out. We spent the rest of the day, Saturday, watching the water slowly receding.

Later on that afternoon, another Army helicopter came overhead. We had made up signs saying "We are staying." One helicopter started to lower down someone to rescue us. But we told them we were OK. It finally became dark and we all fell asleep on the floor.

We awoke Sunday morning to a bright sunshiny day. It was about 7 A.M. The water had receded enough to where we could walk out on the property without wading through water. At the end of the driveway was a brown house that was held in place by a light pole partially on the highway. T.J.'s grocery and gas station was totally destroyed as well as the new Laundromat and Pizza Shop. We went into the store and we got a few bottles of water. I told Paula that we needed to keep track of what we got so I could pay Chuey, the owner for it.

We started on our journey to recover our vehicles. The Tiki Club was destroyed with a yellow house that had floated into it resting at the front door. We could not believe our eyes as to what we were witnessing. We got to Swede's Grocery and it was destroyed. A large blue house was sitting on the highway. We then saw a vehicle coming. They stopped. They said they had broken into the Baptist Church across from Seaside Lumber and rode out the storm there. They said there were 5 people there and a Lion. Mike Kujawa had his grown pet lion at the church with him and the lion was loose in the church. They said Mike put a sign on the church door. It read, "Loose lion in church, Do Not Enter!" Paula and Kenny were going to their property to see what they had left.

We got to the Galveston County Sheriff's office and we found Bill's vehicle at the bottom of the hill with the windshield smashed and all his tools buried in the mud inside the truck. We found my car with a lot of debris on it; another total loss, full of mud and broken windows. We kept on our journey to find Kenny's car which he left parked at the Catholic Church. The church was cut in half at the roof and had at least a dozen destroyed vehicles at the bottom of the hill. The Texas First Bank was half there. There were some houses still standing behind the bank, more than we had seen before, so we thought, maybe this was the worst and things will start getting better.

The Gulf Coast Market was destroyed; but the water slide was still standing. Paula walked down to where her house had been and got upset. She found her daughter's Prom dress in the mud where her house once stood.

Just about that time; a freak thundershower came and we had to take refuge at the entry to Gulf Coast Market. We stayed there until the rain, lightning and thunder quit. Paula and Kenny had walked enough and as they saw they had lost everything, decided to walk back to Murphy's Island. Bill found a bicycle on the side of the road. He tried to ride it. I thought he could ride it to Caplen Shores, but he rode it about a block and was worn out. The wheels were not in the best condition. We left it parked upright on the highway and laughed that someone would come along and see it standing and think it made it through the storm like that.

Bill and I had to keep walking to get to Caplen Shores, where the house was that we were going to stay through the storm was located. We left all my medication, Bill's cell phone, clothes, Sandy's dog and her cat and our cat Fluffy. There used to be a blue dome house in the subdivision. I told Bill that I could see the dome house, so we just knew the house we were to stay in was still there. We got closer and before we knew it we passed the subdivision. There were 10 big houses and there was nothing left in sight. I wanted to cry, but I knew it would upset Bill. I said, "Well there is no reason to walk any further." As I knew our houses in Gilchrist had to be gone, and I was ready to go back.

We started on our 10 mile journey back to Murphy's Island. We were almost to Swede's Grocery and along came and Old red truck. It was occupied by our three Constables, Doug Considine, Rodney Kahla, and William Comeaux. They said, "Stay here and we will be right back to pick you up to take you to Fort Travis for a helicopter to evacuate you from the Peninsula." We stopped by

Murphy's Island and picked up Kenny, Paula and her dogs and Pat Murphy. It was after 5 pm. Doug said they had to be back at their pickup point to take a boat off the Peninsula. We passed the Rancho Carribe Golf Course where our friend Sandy and Bob had stayed. The Pro shop was gone. We just knew they caught a helicopter out the day before.

We got to the Bolivar loop highway and the road was washed out. The Constables got us another ride to Fort Travis and they went to catch their boat off the Peninsula. Pat Murphy was going to his shrimp boat, which he had docked in Bolivar. They told him it was still there and afloat.

We got to Fort Travis and the Galveston Fire Rescue personnel met us at the gate. They said the last helicopter had left for the day, but they would get us another helicopter to take us to a shelter. We waited about a half an hour. While we were standing there I told Bill that it was going to kill me to tell Sandy that her animals were gone. It was at this time that Paula told me that Bob Anderson, (whom was at the Golf Course with Sandy), had told them that Sandy did not make it. A big wave came by and took her. It knocked them down and when he finally got up she was gone. I could not believe that I lost so much in such a short time, but I was glad that we made it through alive.

CNN News came over and interviewed us. They wanted to know why no news media was being allowed on the Peninsula. They were envisioning that there had to be dead bodies everywhere. We told them we walked for 10 miles and never found one body. The helicopter came and got us. They took us to Rice Stadium and then we were put in an ambulance and taken to the George R. Brown Convention Center in downtown Houston.

We walked in and got registered and we went to the restroom to wash off some of the nasty smelling mud we had on us for 3 days. Bill and I tried to get something to eat. I guess I was not that hungry as I could not eat the pasta with tomato sauce on it. The buns were as hard as a rock. We tried to find a pay phone as everyone's cell phone was dead. We found only one and it did not work. We went outside to smoke and never went back in. I knew there was no way I could stay there overnight. It was pretty scary with all of those people that were staying there.

I ran into another Bolivar resident and she let us use her cell phone. I called Julie and Allan, relatives in New Hampshire, the only number I knew by heart, to let them know we were alive. She then let Kenny use her phone to call his dad in north Houston. His dad came and got us within an hour. We showered and went to sleep. The next day, I called friends and family to have them come pick us up.

We will be residing in Magnolia. I will go back to our property to party on Sept 12, 2009 and for future years, but we will never live on the Peninsula again.

Well, it has been almost a year since we lost Sandy. I have been working diligently trying to find her son to get a DNA sample. I finally found him. He is incarcerated in Lancaster, California. I wrote him a letter and I am fervently waiting for his response. I know he had been wondering about his mom but we no longer have a Gilchrist phone so he could not contact us. There is one female body at the Coroner's office and when we get Brian's DNA sample, it will definitely tell us if it is Sandy. If it isn't her, at least they will have her DNA to find her if another body is found. There are 3 women and 1 man that are still missing from the Peninsula. I want to have a Memorial for Sandy, but I want to wait until hopefully we know where her body is at, so we can put her to rest.

Bill and I lived on the Beach about ½ miles from the old Dirty Pelican Pier. We lived there almost 20 years. We stayed for most of the Hurricanes except for Rita and the tropical storms. Tropical storm Francis was the worst. We always got weather reports with an incorrect prediction.

Living on the Peninsula was like living in Paradise. We had two houses and we rebuilt them about 5 times. They were like new houses. New pilings were set up after Hurricane Rita and all new siding and new hurricane windows after Humberto. We worked for 20 years to pay off the houses so that in a couple years we could retire and spend our Golden years fishing.

I managed 5 properties on the Peninsula, but all of these were lost during IKE. No job, no home, no vehicles. When you are 64 years old, it is very hard to believe that you are out in the street. Moving to Houston was not our choice. Living in Houston is quite different from living on the Peninsula with only a couple of stop lights and only one Highway. I could not find work, but a good friend put Bill to work at his company. The recession has now taken his job. I had to file for Social Security and take early retirement. Bill has not made enough for unemployment, so that is all we have.

We were in a FEMA trailer for awhile. That was a nightmare. They came every month to check out the trailer and ask us what our plans were. If you didn't answer them to their satisfaction, they told you they could come and get the trailer at any time. Stress you cannot believe! They offered to let us buy the trailer for $7,000; it only had 2 small bedrooms. They told me, I had to pay Texas sales tax, all insurances, homeowners, wind and flood. It was going to cost $1,200 to move to permanent location and $325.00 month rent. I told them we could not afford anything like that. It would have been about $10,000. It took them less than a week to come and pick up the trailer. At this time we had about $1,000 left. In June I applied for food stamps. As of September 27, 2009 there has been no money, they told me that I qualify and it will just take a couple more days. We are currently staying with a friend that cannot live alone. She also lost her home in Bolivar. Her husband had passed away earlier in the year and last June she lost her daughter. I don't know what we would have done without her.

TWIA, (Texas Windstorm Insurance Agency), paid 11.2% and nothing on contents. I could fix my roof and sheetrock, insulation on house that is no longer there. I am in process of suing them, after paying for insurance for 20 years on 2 houses. There are a few other things that have come into play. Galveston County is now foreclosing for back taxes. If the property is homesteaded, they cannot foreclose, but because I lost my home, I also lost my homestead exemption and now they can take it.

Many people say well, that is what you get for living on the Beach. What they do not realize is there are more than Hurricanes that take away people's existence. Tornados and earthquakes do the same thing. No one could have predicted this storm until it was too late. Crystal Beach and Port Bolivar were not hit as hard as Gilchrist, Texas. I doubt if Gilchrist can ever survive. If you were on the south side of Hwy 87, from High Island to Caplen, you will not be allowed to rebuild. It will just be pretty beaches. There is a property buyout program which is to start in October 2008. It is the only way anyone from this area will be able to recoup some of what they lost.

Galveston is a big tourist attraction and most of the allocated money is going there first. We paid Galveston taxes for all these years and the Peninsula is being treated like a "red-headed step child."

The people that live on the coast are survivors and will continue to do whatever necessary to allow some people to go on living in their Paradise on the Beach.

DAVID AND JANE EWING

"Without God, we would not have made it this far!"

On Wednesday, September 10, 2008, David and Chad, my son, said since the storm was only a Category 2 we would not leave or move our cows. I packed David and myself each three sets of clothes and medicine anyway. Thursday morning at 7:00 A.M. David Edward's of Winnie called David and told him to bring our cattle to Winnie because they had the pens ready. He could not help us because he had to move his own cattle, but he would leave us a truck and trailer to use. David called Chad to help pen them before he went to work. We got all of them penned except 8 cows and 2 heifers. David and I hauled the first load. After unloading them I drove our rig back and David took the other rig. We hauled cows until 4:00 P.M.; then we came home so I could fix supper. David and Chad said if I would take Ruby, David's mother, out they would go stay in Winnie at the Edward's with the cattle. My nephew and his girlfriend lived by the Canal where it floods in a high tide. They did not have a car so I told them to pack their stuff and I would bring them to my house. We had decided to leave early Friday morning.

On Friday morning, around 1:30 A.M., someone from the Sheriff's Office called Chad and told him the water was already over the road at Gilchrist and High Island. If we were going to leave we had to go now! We got up and dressed while David went down to get his mother, Ruby. When they came back we were ready. We got to the beach road when Ruby remembered she had forgotten her false teeth, so I called David as he was in his truck. We were behind him and Chad was behind me. We continued on, slow until he caught back up with us. When we got to Gilchrist there was debris and water all over the road. Rodney Kahla, our deputy, had gone up right before us and he was talking to Chad on the phone telling him what to expect. We had to dodge all kinds of trash on the road. Outside of Gilchrist there was a small red car in the road, with a lady standing outside. She told David she was scared she could not make it through. David told her she didn't have a choice she either had to turn around and go back or get in the line with us. If her car stopped he gave her instruction to grab her purse and get in with one of us. When we got to High Island waves were coming through the dunes. Rodney said to slow down and let the waves pass then go. The water was about three feet deep. I was very scared! At High Island we had to drive up the wrong side because Rodney said the road was washing out on the other side. When we got to the top of the hill we stopped to check our tires, the lady in the red car went around us without a word for saving her life. I was scared and wanted to stay there until day light, but Rodney told us that there was no water on the road or any wind. They would meet us at the Donut Shop in Winnie. When we arrived at the Donut Shop, Our Constables; Doug Considine, William Comeaux and Rodney Kahla were there.

We had just ordered food when Rodney got a call that Kemo had washed off the road and there were more cars behind him. They had to return to High Island to rescue people that couldn't get through.

It seems we were the last people that made it out safely. That shook us up a lot! I decided I would wait for daylight before going on to Woodville. David wanted us to go on. There were two DPS Officers at the station by the Donut Shop. They asked where I was going, when I told them, they checked and said it was clear all the way. Finally, we decided we would go on but then found out I had a flat. David and Chad changed the tire.

When we arrived in Woodville there was a tire shop open so I stopped and had the tire fixed. We finally arrived at Ruby's brother Jake's house. Before we could even take our stuff inside, they informed us that a mandatory evacuation was just issued for Woodville. We called David and told him we were going on to Shelbyville to stay with my cousin, Jo Ann. It was Friday afternoon by the time we arrived. Eddie and Jo Ann sat up and watched the storm but I slept right through it. My alternator went out on my car due to driving through the high waters.

As the days passed we could not get any information as all they talked about was Houston, Galveston and Gilchrist.

No one believed the water would be so bad. Finally, Chad was able to go in to assess the damages. When he called and said, "We had four feet of water in our house and everything was ruined." I cried for days then said, "Things had to go on." David said, "You cannot come back because there was no place to stay." No one really knew how bad things were because they wouldn't let anyone go in. They said Bolivar was gone and bodies were all over. That wasn't true, but there were people that died which they found on Goat Island or across the bay at Oak Island.

On September 21, 2008, Chad called and told us his son, Kenneth had totaled his truck but he was not hurt. The next day I got a call that my last Uncle had passed away. I packed my stuff and took my mother-in-law to Woodville to her brothers Jake's house. She would stay with them for the next two months. I got to Winnie and put Eddie and Chris in a motel paid for by FEMA. After the funeral of my uncle, I moved into the Edward's home with David and Chad. They were very good to us. We can never repay them. After two weeks we bought a camper and moved behind the Winnie Feed Store.

Chad took David down to see things before I could. David told me that he could not even tell where he was when they stopped. Our fences and pens were all gone. All our cows that were left were gone except one that was left in our pasture with no fence. David made the decision to sell all our cattle so we could rebuild.

Once they finally let us all go onto the Peninsula to inspect our homes, we were devastated. After 43 years of marriage, everything was gone except our house. We were blessed because we were able to rebuild.

We called our insurance and they sent someone right away. We were very lucky because we had a good adjuster and we were able to get our money quickly. Of course, it was more than a month before we could start cleaning our house out.

We had to hire a contractor because we had six broken windows. Our contractor came to check in order to give us a bid. It was three weeks before he came back with the bid. Then it took another month before we got the windows put in. We had already cleaned the house and bought the paneling to rebuild but had to wait for the windows. We were driving from Winnie everyday to work on the house. We drove everyday for six weeks. It was very hard because we had to take water and food with us.

Before we could get a permit to rebuild, we had to pay to have our septic tank checked in order to have our electricity redone. It seemed everything was so hard!

On top of all this, every few days my mother-in-law called wanting to come back. Chad was still at the Edward's because he didn't have electricity at his house. He did not have any water damage upstairs.

We finally got electricity the week of Thanksgiving! Chad moved home first and then we moved our camper home.

David and I decided to hire a contractor to fix Ruby's house because she wanted her house fixed first….she did not want to stay with us. She was ninety years old.

We went to Woodville and brought Ruby home for Thanksgiving. She stayed with Chad and cooked for him until she moved back into her home. She moved back into her home on December 20, 2008.

Thanksgiving week we finally got all our windows put in and our utility room put back together. The crew dried in half of it, then left. Our contractor came back and got money from us to buy the siding in order to finish the job. After a month when they didn't return, David finished drying it in and put up the insulation. We had to get a hot water heater and washer and dryer. We had to threaten our contractor with suing him before his crew returned to put on the siding. We had given up on him and hired another contractor to finish the job, when they showed back up. We did use the second contractor to finish the inside of our house. While putting up the plywood on the inside of the utility room they shot four nails into our water pipes. We did not find it until they left. Just one more set back. Nothing came easy!!

We moved back into our home on December 19, 2008, even though the men were just putting in carpet because our daughter and granddaughters were coming for Christmas on that day. We only had beds, stove, refrigerator, washer, dryer, T.V. and David's recliner. We put up a Christmas tree; then went to get a sofa, loveseat and table and chairs the next day.

I didn't mention that my brother Bernard and Shirley were living in a camper in High Island. Every day, when we went to Bolivar we stopped and picked him up a newspaper as there was no delivery there. Bernard and Shirley moved back in time for our family to be together for Christmas.

We thought things were finally turning around when Bernard died, unexpected. That was a terrible blow as we had lost David's sister Janet and my sister, Helen last year. GOD is really testing my faith!

We finally were ready to get our outside blinds. They were ordered then we received a letter saying it would be a delay of four months before we got them. Finally, in July they were installed!

Gradually things are being put back together. Another blow came when we had to have our trees taken down. Our town looks devastated with so many homes gone and very few trees. A lot of friends have passed away and others are having a hard time getting over this.

As soon as I had time, Jean and I started getting our Methodist Church back together. We had carpet donated; then a man donated to the church some money so we used it to get new windows for the back part. The same man sent another man down to install us a new air conditioner. A church in Houston donated to our church, pews and an alter. Our church is the only one usable in Port Bolivar, so we are sharing it with the Baptists and Catholics. We are very fortunate that High Island shares their Pastor, Marty Boddie, with us. Without GOD, we would not have made it this far!

A year later, we finally have a new porch and steps for our utility room. They were given to us by some FEMA workers. Now all we need are garage doors.

A special thanks to Rodney Kahla, without him, I don't know if we would have made it this far!!

JOHN JASON COOK

"There is something about the ocean with its constant movement and its blank entirety that makes me feel as if I were looking at eternity. My mind begins to mingle with the movement, the sound, the smell, always moving toward eternity. I could feel the hand clench the emptiness of myself as it begins to loosen. I looked and looked at the ocean. My faith, my church...and after awhile....peace.

The Stairs remained

Photo taken by Barry Haley

On Friday, September 12, 2008

The tide surges that I expected would have been 6 – 8 feet in a Category 2 storm. I was expecting them to arrive early that evening. However the tide surges started around mid-afternoon (3:00 P.M.). No rain, no wind at that time. I was in the house when I heard the waves under the house. I went outside on the deck and could see waves breaking under the house. I started down the stairs and looked to see my truck was under water and the garage/workshop/ laundry room had about 3 feet of water in it. I waded through the water into the work area to put what I could on high ground (shelves, elevated tables, work bench.) I went back upstairs, set on the deck and watched the water recede. I sat there for a couple of hours watching minor tide surges come in. Just before dark a major surge came in, it washed away the dunes in front of the first house; the dunes were 5 – 6 feet with heavy vegetation. My house was 4th row back from the beach. It started to rain, not much, but the wind also began to pick up and it was dark by now. Around 10:30 P.M. I went back outside to check the downstairs, the truck was totally covered, all of the downstairs was gone; all the walls and everything inside. Everything, the only thing left was the slab and pilings. I went back upstairs to check for leaks or damage. About an hour or so the waves were breaking on the deck. My house was 12 feet off the ground. Normally riding out a category 2, I would expect 6′ – 8′ waves… this was now more like 12′- 15′! My deck started to break loose from the house, just as it washed away the wind lifted up the north corner of the roof, breaking away ½ of the roof. Rafters fell into the kitchen. At this time there was no water in the house, but shortly after, half the other part of the roof started to cave in. The east wall was the 1st to go from the water, then the north wall, then the south wall (front of house facing beach). By this time I am trying to get to the roof, I am standing on my chair and the water is chest high. I pulled myself up through a hole into the crawl space that soon starts to collapse. I manage to get on the section of the roof that has the metal fireplace stack. That section of the roof finally starts to float away. It is so dark that I don't know where I am going, but I am above water. I floated about six+ hours until I hit some land. I was floating on a piece of the roof, hanging onto the metal chimney stack for these 6+ hours. It was like being inside of a blackball, an 8 ball, I guess. At one point I was above myself looking down at myself…I could see myself!!?… Clearly, then I was back on the roof holding on the chimney stack. During the ride, I managed to reach down into the water and I found a wet jacket that I used to cover myself. It is still dark, but I can see land, I am still on the roof and debris is between me and land, so I start to crawl across what is floating to reach land. I reach a 12 feet piece of beach and a steep bank. It is still raining and the wind is blowing. I climbed the bank, no lights, nothing. I lie down and cover myself with the jacket and I went to sleep.

Saturday, September 13, 2008

After a few hours of sleep, I wake up and it is still raining and blowing wind. It is so dark, I cannot see my hand. I lie back down and go to sleep. I wake up later and it is starting to clear, still raining but the wind has dropped off. When daylight came upon me, I managed to find a big green trash bin and I got inside it to cover my body with only my feet hanging out in the rain. By the way, with the day light, I could see the jacket that I was using to cover myself…it was my father's police jacket. I do not know where I ended up, but I was on land. I start moving, marsh on one side, bay or gulf on the other side. I am on a spine of high ground, very thick vegetation all shin deep. I move for several hours, nothing to be seen. Finally I move down to a very small beach. I had tried to alert the choppers that flew over with a strobe light that was in a pocket. No luck. I could see so many helicopters flying over me, but they could not see me! After I got down to the beach, debris was everywhere. There was 6' – 8' high trash; nothing but trash. I was looking in the trash to see what I could use. I found a skim board, but could not get it loose from the trash. I turned around and saw a bright orange life-vest. I put it on and the next chopper I saw was an Air Force Rescue. They picked me up and took me to a hospital. The hospital treated me and then sent me to a shelter. At the evacuation shelter the only thing I had to wear was the hospital gown, no clothes, no identification; I had nothing! I had to beg for a blanket and when I got one, it was so rough, stiff and scratchy. From this center, two of my kids picked me up and took me to their house in Dallas.

I sit and think about what I lost because of Hurricane IKE. I lost my house and everything in it, my pets (3 cats and 1 dog). I tried to get them, but the house was coming apart too fast. They are terrified!!…they are lost, not to be replaced. Puppy (her name), she was dropped off at my fireworks stand on July 4, 2000, I took her home. Jeanine, my lovely wife, said we had to take her to an adoption center in Galveston, but because of the Holidays they were closed for 4-5 days. Jeanine did not want to name her; she said if we named her we would become too attached. We already had a chow mix dog that Jeanine had rescued off of the beach in 1991. Now, this dog we never took to the adoption center, her name is Puppy, whom was half black German shepherd and coyote…turned out to be a good mix!! Jeanine died On November 3, 2003 and Sandy Standridge and I got together 9 months after that. The year 2004 we were all very happy!! The year 2008 sucked, Sandy died on May 10, 2008.

Oh, just a note only 4 people ever touched, Puppy, the vet Jeanine, Sandy and I. Then IKE; I lost the house, everything in it, including the pets, Puppy, Danny, Christen, MR. and BK. I also lost my truck, my identification; the only thing left is an empty sand lot. In four years I lost everything, Jeanine, Sandy, our home, our pets and one red truck. I am now living in an apartment in Dallas, and I make frequent trips back to Crystal Beach.

ANNE OSTEN CHRISTIAN AND LIZ OSTEN SANDERS

"Remembering the Seahoose"

Bop's house...
"The SEAHOOSE"

was here

Before and After of the Seahoose

The one year marker of the last day I spent at The Seahoose in Crystal Beach, Texas, exacerbated by the anniversary of 9/11 the day before, and what would have been Mama's 85th Birthday 4 days prior to that.

Last Saturday was a stormy morning in Houston, the skies eerily similar to the year before, and I was feeling particularly blue. It was my intention to recount the days following IKE, but I now know the stories I want to tell are not about the loss of, but the life of The Seahoose.

My mind is flooded with ideas, I wish I could sit and write full time as I am excited for the first time since having to leave the beach.

My brother, Tom took over crystalbeach.com just a few weeks before Mama passed away unexpectedly in her sleep on March 22, 2007. After the storm, in the blink of an eye everything on the site was suspended in limbo.

There is little information coming out about the status of Bolivar Peninsula. We would later learn it was because it was still under water, and the authorities were trying to assess the loss of life before allowing anyone over there.

Tom created a page for people to share stories about the beach while we all waited for news.

Our beloved Seahoose is gone, there is nothing but sand left in its place. It had a ramp for Dad's (Bop) wheelchair with a concrete statue of Mary at the top. It had a white washed picnic table that family and friends had signed and/

or etched their words of wisdom. Mama and Bop had 7 children; the Osten's to date count 48.

It hosted many a spaghetti dinner for all the pot would feed. Bop always made "Character Sauce," mushrooms, onion, "Rotel" tomatoes and fresh jalapenos, so named for what it required to eat it.

The Seahoose witnessed countless games of poker, dominoes, and hearts; so many crowded around the glass table, often into the wee hours of the night. Mama and Bop slept through the noise as if it were a lullaby.

The picture of us at our tacky party hung next to those from the Mardi Gras parades, when we were 101 Dalmatians with Cruella, and Charlie Chaplins and Waldos – we won first place once. Next in line was the Bay Vue first dollar, followed by the framed traffic ticket Bop got in France for going the wrong way in the circle, at the end the picture of Bop with the caption "it's not so much I mind dying, it's just I don't want to be there when it happens."

Bop spent many hours in his shop working with stained glass and his beautiful creations hung in all of our windows. Bop and Annie painted the little kitchen table with neon paint and glued fish pictures on it they had cut out of one of the coffee table books. We never had a true coffee table, but Mama had lots of beautiful coffee table books about the sea. They painted the fan blades to match. Actually anything that stood still was at risk of being painted, just ask Felix, our 18 pound black cat.

This was our HOME, not a vacation getaway. How many people sat on the porch swing in 34 years? Is it more or less than the number of shark teeth in the baby food jar on the kitchen window sill found over the same amount of time? How many grand kids got in Mama and Bops' king size bed to watch Disney videos on the television suspended from the ceiling? More than the family and friends who, in our 1200 square feet house, looked for their floor space assignment on the nightly bed chart over the year? It is too late to calculate now.

In recent years Annie and I spent hours combing the beach for glass and tile. Sorted and saved for projects never started, I guess it was really all about the hunt. Our stash has been returned for others to find.

When we were young we had a 400 feet seine and we would have fish fry's on the beach with our catch. Our "plate" was a brown paper bag, the fish seasoned with just the right amount of sand to ensure peak crispiness. The kids would throw the crabs back, so many pinched fingers! Anheuser Busch bought several Clydesdale horses with the money we spent on beer, perhaps one was Hank.

In our haste to follow the last minute evacuation order, we forgot to bring Bop's poker fund jar, and Rick's poker fund jar, and Liz's poker fund kept in the Halloween purse on the bed post with the "keeper" Mardi Gras beads; Hama's, (Bops' grandmother), Santa so prominently displayed on the Christmas tree every year, and the 4 feet turquoise pre-lit metal Christmas tree with a tilt. We didn't forget, but we were forced to leave, damn near everything else.

Bop and Mama moved to Crystal Beach in 1974 and ran the Bay Vue Grocery until 1983. Then they started Mike (Mama's nickname) Osten Real Estate, (M.O.R.E.) when forced to give up the real estate business due to health reasons in 1990, Mama created the crystalbeach.com website to provide information about her community to those surfing the net. She was 72 years old. Mama would spend at least 6 hours a day updating the site and answering all inquiries.

Mama and Bop loved Crystal Beach as did the other 46 of us and many, many friends. We scattered Mama's ashes on the dune in front of the Seahoose in March of 2007. IKE may have washed away the dune, but it only served to widen her presence on this place she treasured.

The Osten family will be back soon, but not as soon as we would like. There are too many memories to mention, too many laughter filled times, to recall. She was a grand ole house, The Seahoose, and we will miss her. And maybe, just maybe years from now, a treasure will be found buried in the sand by some unknowing hunter…a concrete statue of the Blessed Mary.

On September 12, 2008, there were 16 projected paths on Stromtracker, one a direct hit on Galveston, my research showing it had been the most accurate over the past few days, which put the "dirty" and most devastating side over Bolivar. The news continued to predict a last minute turn to the south, and reiterated it was "only a Cat. 2," I knew in my heart this was going to be the one!!

So many close calls over so many years can make one reluctant to respond, Gustav just 3 weeks earlier, you find that you tell yourself, "It is going to be OK."

The mandatory evacuation was ordered, the Ferry would stop running at 11:00 P.M., and they wanted us out by 3:00 P.M.

There was a woman and child at the water's edge, the child romping in the surf like any other beach morning, momentarily fooling me into thinking this was just like any other day. Sadly the feeling was gone as quickly as it was felt, the reality was I had to get organized, make a plan, and get my family out of our beloved Seahoose as fast as I could.

By 8:00 A.M., the tide water was up the road level with our house. Although at this point we were protected by substantial dunes built for many decades and enhanced by our Mama's presence, the early arrival of the effects was sobering.

It was too late to go for a trailer or U-haul and return, pack it and leave on time. We spent the morning trying to decide what few things to take that would represent the lifetime of family memories present in the Seahoose.

So many, many storms in the past, the family would rally and come in their vehicles to help save what we could. This time it was too late; Liz, Bop and I were on our own.

We had the Trailblazer and my Saturn to load. We first loaded the wheelchair, walker, potty chair and medical supplies; all absolutely vital for Bop's well being. Then next we packed the suitcase with clothes for each of us. We did a very poor job here though, Liz forgot all shoes, but the ones she had on, we only packed three days of changes for Bop and I forgot to open my shorts drawer all together. I thought and believed we'd be home in a few days! Next the family photo albums, Bible, Bop's old scrapbooks, the framed Bay Vue first dollar, the ticket from France, some of Mama and Bop's creations, and after that my mind goes blank. There was so much, the Seahoose was crammed full of 35 years of collections, treasures, each thing triggering a special memory, but the clock was ticking, it was absolutely necessary we consider Bop's safety above anything else!

I had boarded up, (and thankfully un-boarded), the house myself 3 weeks earlier, for Gustav, so I was confident I could handle it this time. I hadn't considered what a challenge it would be to handle the 4x8 sheets of plywood in the wind, another sobering reminder of what was very different this time and its possible outcome. Screws didn't drive so easily, probably my stress and exhaustion more than anything else. I used big nails for the ones that I couldn't drive the screws through, leaving the patio door open until it was time to leave.

We cleared the deck completely and laid Mama's concrete statue of the Blessed Mary on her back. Surely she would make it, she weighed a ton!

Then there were 3 cats; Felix, Ditto and P-Kitty. I wrestled with my conscience all day, if IKE did go south, they would be OK boarded up in the house, this was what I told myself to override what my heart was telling me…that they would be killed when the house was blown away by the wind and/or washed away in the storm surge. I accepted this fate easily for the outside strays Liz had adopted and fed for years; but our cats, what should I do? I was the driving force, the rational one and in charge; it was my role. They were comforted by this, and it's what I have always done. But, with the vehicles packed to capacity, and evacuating to the Winnie motel room, how reasonable was it to take the cats with us? In the scheme of things they were our kitties, but they weren't human life and I had to accept they were disposable.

I shot pictures of the inside of the house and decided to do the outside right before we left thinking it may be important for the insurance process. While shooting I realized it would be nice to show Bop's website fans from where he shot his morning post, as it was a very real possibility it would be gone this time, and with it, life as we knew it. After uploading the photo I moved on and FORGOT to put Mama and Bop's computers in the car, so we lost the history of pictures forever. I can't believe I did that, why didn't I think more clearly?

As we got the cars loaded, we had heard that the water was already washing over Rollover Pass. It was time to go whether or not we were ready. Bop and Liz in the Trailblazer, I filled a huge bowl with water and another with kitty food and then I had to drive huge nails to hold the last piece of plywood over the patio door.

The drive to Winnie was uneventful, we got Bop settled into the hotel room, and we were surrounded by fellow beach folks. My mind racing as to what we needed to be comfortable, I realized we never considered food, so I hit the local gas stations and paid a fortune for peanut butter, crackers, chips, candy, water and beer. We watched the news all evening and it became apparent our worst fear would very likely be realized.

The cats gnawed at my conscience all evening, I could not live with my decision! I talked to my daughter, Molly around 10:00 P.M. about the guilt. I knew I had already decided to go back and get them but presented it as an idea. She made me promise not to go alone, she knew I wouldn't promise NOT to go, so it was, "Please MOM, don't go alone!" There was no other way though, Bop couldn't be left alone. I can't recall another time I knowingly broke a promise to Molly, but there was no other way. I had gotten three boxes to put them in, and at 11:00 P.M. set out for the Seahoose.

My heart pounding for 40 miles, I was blessed not to encounter any high water. Once at the house, the wind was incredible, it was eerie, no one around, the surf was pounding, the water creeping up higher and higher into the neighborhood. Standing on the deck I remembered having to nail the board that would let me in. I finally managed to pull the nails on one side allowing me to squeeze through and into the quiet of our beloved house.

One by one I boxed the cats, pushing the plywood open enough to squeeze me and a box through and took them to my car. I wish I had stopped to think about grabbing some of my precious treasures that never entered my mind that busy day. Little Si – one of Liz's strays, and by far one of the most ignorant cats I have ever encountered was huddled on the deck. I opened a can of wet cat food and gave her the whole thing, a real treat for her, it was her last meal after all, and she may as well gorge herself.

I got the plywood nailed back in place, and I sat quietly on the deck and took in what I could. This place, this magnificent place, even in its fury it was so beautiful. It is all of the smells of the salt air and the sounds of the surf. I turned back and looked at the house, trying to etch everything I could into my brain, every inch. Reality nudged me; I had to go, NOW!

The meowing was amazingly loud, a three-some serenade that fueled my anxiety. Thankfully, Felix, our 20+ black cat clawed his way out of the box in less than 3 minutes, P-Kitty in the next 2 minutes. The kitty screaming let up, except for poor little Ditto, she never figured out how to get out of that box and quietly meowed the whole way.

I made it back to Winnie by the Grace of God. Bop didn't know I had left; we didn't want to worry him. He was comforted to have the cats in the room, we were all together again. My day finally completed, I turned to the television again and the torturous waiting....for our uninvited guest, IKE!

The collections inside the Seahoose

WILL RANEY

"Billy-Bad-Bird"

"Hello everyone – I am Billy-bad-bird!" 7 days ago, I woke up to a gigantic wave of water smashing through the front of my house and into my bedroom where I was tossed around like a leaf blowing in the air. I escaped through my window where the oceans fury had taken my neighborhood. My neighbor's houses were gone and the pets they left behind were clinging to milk crates and floating debris. I called for them to please come – please come and they tried, but they got scared. I watched them drown, before my very eyes and this haunted me when I got to the Highway trying to make it to the bunkers at Fort Travis.

Fort Travis is where I have weathered all the many storms everyone knows I so love. The ocean was crashing through the levies, some waves were twenty feet, they would knock me down and I would scream, "LORD, PLEASE!" I would get up and another wave and another…they just kept coming! My prayers could not, not stop the waves. I felt like those trapped dogs, I had seen earlier, I just wanted to turn around and go back to get them, but I could not, I had to force myself to move on. I was wearing boots, but I let them go to save my life. I tried to climb a speed limit sign but that too was engulfed. I saw a large tree lying in the road and I made it and climbed over it and took a half second rest because the Fort was in sight. However, the road was getting deeper and deeper! There WAS a grocery store, with a two story hotel which became my new plan of action. I nearly drowned getting to the second floor. When I did get there, I had only 6 steps left not underwater, yet the wind was behind me and the rain behind me too. I sat down, with my head between my knees. It was me and a stray cat further down the hall. We knew each other were there; we would ride this out together. I knew I was okay, "thank you Lord, oh my God, Thank you Lord for letting me live through this!" I did not know what time it was…I knew that at 2:00 A.M., I would see the "eye", that is what time I figured it was when the winds starting screaming…when the water rose higher than the balcony….when I started screaming…. "Lord, please, Lord, please!?" Holding onto each door handle that would snap under the concrete beam…no longer holding together the concrete roof that was bending while I moved to the next beam….then the next! Until I was no longer under the concrete roof…I feared it would collapse on me….until it stopped and I saw a full moon and I prayed again, "Oh my God, my God…thank you, thank you!" Until the second eye wall came in with a fury and a wall of water that engulfed me and the whole 50 feet that it knocked me…and then I did not pray the words…please Lord, save me again…I only prayed for Heaven, "Please Lord, let my life be heaven…life was not important any longer…heaven was all I wanted!" Suddenly the windows blew out, I jumped into safety and my feet are still full of glass to prove it. Hours later, when it was calm, I left the bathroom where I hid and opened the door to see Mr. Cat, who ran under the bed and stayed there the same two days as I….waiting for the water to recede. On the third day, I went out in search for food! I found only a can of sardines which went to the cat. On the fourth day, I made it down the highway to a school and slept on the back balcony in wet clothes under a beautiful full moon! On the fifth day, I made it closer to my parent's house…but before I got there, I was picked up by a friend, who had a lion with a story to tell far greater than mine!!! We were met by the military, with guns drawn…they were giving us orders to find a way out or the lion would be shot and we would be shot too. Helicopters came from everywhere, millions of them, everyone trying to see the lion. Suddenly, the military got scared and all who were mean became friends without choice. It had been six days without food and water. The helicopters brought MRE's, (meals ready to eat), water and coke. Everywhere I went I had 50 military follow and every time I heard a cat or a dog I went in search of it. When I found them I fed them a MRE and when I saw a dead cat or dog, (still chained to a tree), I would let out a "wail." I sat and cried and cried! The soldiers who watched the last cat eat and watch me bust open a street lamp to make a bowl for water…they came and picked up the cat….they petted the cat and kissed the cat and told me the cat had a home. When I first met the soldiers, it was the rifles pointed at me from 100 directions, then it was with a bottle of water, then they asked my name, and I told them, "Will…but everyone calls me Billy." They didn't get to ask why before I found a big bag of Cheetos and yelled, "BIRD", I threw the Cheetos on the ground and a million seagulls came from nowhere, they ate so quietly. I threw another bag and another bag, and told them, "I have to go now…but daddy will be right back! We are going to fix this and get our life like it was before!" The soldiers just stood there, never said another word. We got the lion in the cage and the tiger, too and a 40 caravan escort out of town. One soldier shook my hand, and said, "Billy, you're one bad bird!"…and I replied, "Yes, but I ain't no bad bird, that's just my name!"

A pile of debris

RUSTY AND SARAH STANDRIDGE

"If we struggle against the waves that pass over us in life, we are overpowered. If we swim with the waves in life as they rollover us, the waves pass on."

Sarah, Rusty and Randy trying to get our 4 dogs towards the Black Hawk

Just days before the storm, Rusty and I had spent Monday and Tuesday driving to Orlando, Florida to attend the Surf Expo Trade Show to purchase products for Latitude 29.2 Surf Shop for the 2009 season. On Wednesday, September 10, 2008 we were starting to get panicked phone calls from Kimberly at the store, friends and family regarding the dangerous Hurricane IKE. We watched the Orlando news nervously at the hotel and it was still showing Hurricane IKE as a Category 2 heading towards Corpus Christi. We were very confused as we kept getting more and more phone calls about a mandatory evacuation on the Bolivar Peninsula.

Finally, one of our dog sitters, Jason, calls as he is getting ready to prepare to evacuate with all four of our dogs to San Antonio. We freaked out knowing he would not be able to manage a road trip with our four big hyper dogs! We had to act!! At 7:00 P.M., Wednesday, September 10th, Rusty and I discussed the situation; we called Jason and Kimberly back and told them we were on our way back to Crystal Beach to get our puppies. We checked out of the hotel and we were on the "road again" by 7:30 P.M, another 1000+ miles! We drove straight through the night and arrived back in Crystal Beach at 9:30 A.M., Thursday, (as everyone else was evacuating), to rescue our dogs!

By this time, the radio stations were announcing that anyone remaining on the Bolivar Peninsula, "May Face Certain Death." We made it to our home, checked on the pups, started boarding up the stores and loading up the vehicles. We inquired with the police about the latest we could leave and we were told we **had** to be off the peninsula before noon on Friday. We continued to work like maniacs securing everything, with no sleep for nearly 48 hours, we finally, exhausted crashed around 6:00 P.M. Thursday evening.

On Friday, September 12, 2008 Rusty and I awoke around 2-3 A.M., made coffee and went out on the deck to talk and to make plans. As we were talking and awakening, there was a full moon and there was a reflection towards the front row beach houses down from us…we kept looking at it…it was still night and dark…we basically stopped communicating!! We were still so tired and plain out exhausted we didn't want to imagine the worst, what we thought it was, but we knew inside our hearts!! It was 16 hours before the storm was to hit us, we were already trapped!! Franticly, we called friends we knew were planning to leave Friday morning also. We were all stranded; they had already checked the escape routes, there were none!!

We met with Barry Hailey and lots of other folks at his Super Mini Storage Units, (his building was built to withstand 200 mph winds), and we kind of felt safe with that. Soon the water starting coming up through his drain in his field and we all thought that was odd!! Within 30 minutes the Gulf was coming into his parking lot and it was flowing fast!! Then all of the streets perpendicular to the ocean were becoming rivers onto Highway 87. We all decided we needed to get to a concrete fixture, if we were going to live!! (And at this point and time, we had doubts! It was serious!!) This was about 8:30 A.M. on Friday. The safest places appeared to be either Coconuts Restaurant or the Crenshaw Elementary School. I had already parked my vehicle at the First Baptist Church, it was higher ground. Rusty left with the dogs for the school. I rode with Brant and his car starting taking water in, it became submerged in the water! Two of us girls, pushed the car out of the 3-4 feet water, adrenal going or what!? We went to the school and met with 25-30 others already there. It was strange we had a chance to let our puppies roam on leashes underneath the school. Then all of sudden and quickly the water started coming upon the back fields of the school and then engulfed the underneath of the school. Of course, by this time, dozens and dozens of phone calls had been made since 3:00 A.M. for help.

However, there was a huge oil barge loaded with people and lots of oil getting ready to crash on the peninsula, so the coast guard was busy helping and doing all they could do! We finally got the coast guard helicopters and it was a group decision, families with children go first!

Around 10:00 A.M., the National Guard came down in front of Crenshaw Elementary School on Highway 87 with 4 (four) huge black hawk helicopters to rescue us!! It was an awesome, but a terrifying sight! Rusty and Barry had taken down the street signs and laid them neatly to the side of the road for the helicopters to land, so after the storm they could restore them. No one thought, it was going to be this bad! Rusty and I had been so isolated from the reality of this dangerous storm; being in Florida, then driving and not being able to watch the news! Anyway, the best decision Rusty and I have ever made; we came back and rescued Roxy, Charlie, Lattie and Samantha from the storm. In the meantime, we had been avoiding the 20+ phone calls from Dad and Mom! We were hoping they would think we were still safe in Florida and we did not want them to worry about us. I finally called them around 9:30 A.M. and told them we were awaiting a helicopter to get off of the peninsula. Now, they were worried!

There was so much confusion with the helicopter landing and everyone scurrying around, trying to get our frightened dogs towards the helicopters was not at all easy. Rusty had to pick up our 100+ pound Chocolate Lab, Roxy, and throw her into the helicopter. Our helicopter had about 6 dogs, 3 cats and 12 humans and believe it or not the dogs and cats all got along!! We left behind, Al and Mary against our will to ride out the storm; they did not want to come with us!

I will never forget Ralph, driving his jeep up the front concrete stairs of the school…he did it 3 times, (scary, we just knew he was going to flip over), until he finally made it all the way up. The whole crowd watching and then applauding with relief, when he made it!! We were the last grouping off the peninsula, the wind was picking up strongly and we had a hard time getting up in the air. When we did get in the air, we looked down below through the helicopter windows and the entire peninsula was submerged by the Gulf. It was then that I realized I had left my purse with all of my I.D.'s and money in the back of Barry's pick-up truck. There was nothing I could do, but consider it was gone! However, I did hope that Al and Mary might see it and try to save it!

The National Guard dropped us off at the Gray Hound Park in Texas City. At this point, Rusty and I are trying to find a rental car, a taxi or even a car dealership. Of course, everything was closed for evacuation. We ended up, against our will, taking the evacuation bus to wherever with our four dogs which we had to muzzle to get onto the bus to start the journey! Eight hours later, we arrived at a school in Austin and all of the cots were full. We journeyed to 2 more schools and they were also full! There was no place to go, except stay in the bus. Luckily, just out of the blue, our sales representatives, Jeff and Katy Hammett, called us and they lived in Austin. Jeff came and picked us up, (Randy, Ralph, Rusty, Sarah and our 4 dogs.) They had even boarded up their dogs so that our dogs could stay in their yard!! We arrived at their house around 10:00 P.M., exhausted from the day of events. Jeff and Katy gathered up toothbrushes, clothes and bedroom slippers for us! I called my parents to let them know we were safe, (it was probably midnight their time), but I don't think they would have slept until I called. We went to bed…not sleep, but we were in bed, tossing and turning. My cell phone rings at 3:00 A.M., it is Lacy, (Rusty's little brother's girlfriend), she is panicked that Lee is missing. He was out on a boat with two friends trout gigging, the boat capsized and he never surfaced!? At this point, we had the speculation that we had lost everything and then possibly a life on top of it all!

On Saturday, September 13, 2008, we woke up at Jeff and Katy's house and it wasn't a bad dream, it was an actual reality that we did not want to comprehend. We had coffee and stayed glued to the news station and monitored the computer for any news about the Hurricane. We also kept in close touch with Lacy about any news on Lee. The news media was actually still talking about Katrina and the "likeness"!! By late Saturday morning, the news finally reported that, "THE BOLIVAR PENINSULA IS GONE!" We were shocked and questioned what the media meant. We were hoping and praying that what we had just heard was wrong.

Jeff and Katy were generous to let us borrow their vehicle to roam around Austin. We had to get away from the media and we needed clothes. We could only take one small tote per person with us on the helicopter. We had to leave everything else behind.

Sharon Brandt, an adopted family member, was worried sick about us. Sharon insisted on picking us up and staying with her in Round Rock, TX and we took her up on it. She picked us up in this little Lexus car; we had 4 big scared dogs, 3 human bodies and our backpacks. It was extremely funny with all of us in this car and the looks other drivers were giving us. If only we had been in the spirit to laugh more, it was a great moment!!

On Monday, September 15, 2008, we got the phone call, the search was over; they had found Lee's body.

While we were at Sharon and Brad's home, the news flashed about going to the Convention Center for help from the FEMA and the Red Cross. We borrowed their vehicle and traveled 39 miles to the Austin Convention Center. When we got there, we waited in the American Red Cross Line. When it was our turn, they laughed at us and told us that it looked like we had just walked out of the "RITZ HOTEL." Go figure that one out; we were wearing shorts, t-shirts and flip-flops!

Rusty and I had been trying to look for a vehicle on Craig's List and in the newspaper; but it was too overwhelming and extremely too hard to focus. Brad and Sharon had been planning to sell their 2001 Ford Expedition; it was perfect timing and so easy to buy the vehicle in the driveway. The next day, Brad was all excited with his new red truck!! Additionally, we had been talking about all of the journeys with 4 dogs. We knew it was going to be hard to find a place to stay with *so* many dogs. Brad and Sharon had been considering getting a companion for Gabrielle, their Dalmatian. Charlie was our newest adoptive dog to our family; he is an overly affectionate collie puppy. We felt like we had saved Charlie from the streets and then from Hurricane IKE and now he was in a good home with a doggie door! Some of the stories of Charlie, he is so full of personality. One short tale, he realized that he could take Sharon and Brad's new sofa pillows outside through this doggie door!

48

The waiting for the authorities to let us go back to our property seemed like years, but it was only 2 weeks and a day. The unknowing of all and the boredom of waiting for the unknown drove us crazy! After 2 weeks, on Friday, September 26th, we were finally allowed onto the Peninsula. We waited in the long line on Highway 124 for hours until we made it to the check point. Our local police were there and they just waved us on. As we turned onto Highway 87, what we saw was beyond devastating! It was something we could never picture in our lifetime. There were cars and trucks tossed and crushed everywhere, parts of houses tossed everywhere, houses ripped wide open, houses barely standing, tons and tons of debris everywhere and then there were areas where there was absolutely nothing left. Words cannot even begin to describe it; it was terrible and it hurt!

We drove through Crystal Beach and stopped at our store, Latitude. At this point and time, we were too mentally gone and too devastated to even touch anything. All we could do was try to absorb with our eyes. Rusty tended to the funeral arrangements on September 27th and after a 2nd visit to the Peninsula on September 28th we bolted to South Carolina, (1000 miles), to my parents!!

My parents helped to save our sanity; Rusty and I needed their stability and their strength to make it!! That Sunday, October 5, 2008, we went to the 1st Presbyterian Church with my parents and David Renwick's sermon was on "Experiencing God: The Crisis of Belief," we were in tears, it was like his sermon was focused on us and he was talking directly to us. Later, David told my parents, that he plans the sermons months in advance and he could not believe this "one special sermon" fell on Rusty and my first Sunday in the church. Of course, the entire congregation knew my parents children lived in Crystal Beach and they had been concerned for our well-being and of our hardships.

Rusty and I drove the S.C. trip, (2000 miles round trip), probably more than 2 dozen times "to get that spiritual-parental guidance," over the crucial periods from September 2008 until March 2009!! Everyone questioned our long and frequent journeys, but when we would come back from Mom and Dad's refreshed and in better spirits, they understood and were in awe!!!

In October, during one of our trips in South Carolina, we purchased a 28 foot camper to bring back to Crystal Beach, TX. It was an experience, especially in the Atlanta, GA traffic, but we managed to make it to the Texas State line Welcome center. The Bolivar Peninsula was under curfew; residents were only allowed to enter between 6:00 A.M. until 2:00 P.M., so we transferred from the Expedition to the Camper and we spent our first night in the camper at the Welcome center. I think it was a bit confusing for our pups, (Roxy, Lattie and Samantha), and they panicked at every noise! We didn't sleep very well either; there were a lot of noisy folks in the Welcome Center parking lot! I kept wondering if they were doing the same thing that we were doing. At 4:00 A.M., we started for the Peninsula and made it to the check-point a few minutes before 6:00 A.M., he let us go on through! Once, in Crystal Beach, Rusty pulled into the Tiki Bar parking lot, (which was right across the street from our store), we stayed there until daylight. When it became daylight, we were planning to move the camper and set up behind our store. Around, 8:00 A.M. Chris Gatlin, the owner, saw us and offered us a spot right in the front of the Tiki to "camp out." This became our homestead for the next 5 months. It was actually a wonderful place; the Tiki was one of the community gathering spots. The owners, Chris and Karen Gatlin made it a very welcoming place to all. We were constantly around people and seeing lots of buddies for the first time since the storm. It was crazy; our residents were all so displaced in San Antonio, Dallas, Port Lavaca, Beaumont, Winnie, etc. The Church of Christ Building was completely gone; only a slab remained. However, By mid October, Jerry and Debbie Valentine, started having their Sunday morning church services at the Tiki. It was awesome and it was much needed!

Latitude 29.2 Surf Shop

By mid October, we had started getting our outside property "kind of" cleaned; there was just so, so much debris! Our store was still partially standing, but it looked like a bomb had been set off in it!! At times, we wished that it had just been completely wiped away; it would have been less to deal with!! We slowly started knocking it out; some days we spent all day and then other days 1 hour was all we could handle. We were faced with the mud, the rotted clothes, the mold, the rusted racks, snakes, parts of other houses and decking; they had all been swirled around into a creation of a tangled mess. We were hearing that most of our inventory was across the bay on Goat Island! The images of the store, like a huge 10 feet fish aquarium, and our inventory being scattered miles away during the storm. We managed to salvage some wetsuits, life-vest, kayaks and surfboards; only to have these all looted away from us! By this point, we had been through so much and people were stealing what little bit we had left. The looting was so way out of hand and so uncontrollable by the few wonderful police on the Peninsula. It was just too much for any of us to handle!

Our house was still standing, but in a serious "ICU" condition. We had a huge 25 feet wide and 10 feet deep sink-hole underneath the bedroom section, underneath the concrete foundation and we were missing 4 pilings. Of course, the entire underneath was wiped away and both of our decks, the elevator and stairs were completely gone. It was interesting trying to get into our house; the main entrances are 12 feet high on pilings. We just knew the sink hole was going to get larger and our house would get pulled into it. The bedroom was like a trampoline when we tried to walk on it, so we didn't walk on it much! We hired a group to start working on it and let them stay in the house, without water and electricity, while they did the work.

In the midst of all of this, towards late November, Rusty started getting disturbing phone calls from his older brother, Tommy. It was non-sense talk, and eventually the harsh words were pushed to the side. On December 10th, 2008 we will never forget, it snowed! Rusty was exhausted from "all" and now the everyday drives to Beaumont to visit Tommy in the hospital. That evening I went outside of the camper by myself, (Rusty was a sleep), and I knew and sensed it was some sort of a message for it to snow in Crystal Beach! The next morning/day on December 11, 2008, Rusty and I witnessed 8+ hours of Tommy, Jr., struggling to breathe until the end of his life!! Our entire life just kept crumbling on us! Not only did "Hurricane IKE" destroy us, but we had just lost 3 members of the family in 7 months. Somehow Rusty managed; our sanity was definitely up for major questioning!

We spent the holidays in South Carolina with my parents and family, it was great moments! We were there, however it was a blur! It didn't feel like a time to celebrate Thanksgiving or Christmas. It was just a wonderful "break" being with the family, having fun and being able to temporarily forget and not deal with the destruction of our lives in Texas.

The first of the New Year, we were determined that 2009 had to be a better year! We finally got water to the house right after Christmas and we had a temporary electrical pole set. We were making progress!! By now, the camper was getting smaller and smaller and even our dogs were becoming cranky! It became an every night ritual of having to "bully" the pups for a seat in the camper!! We finally told the workers at our house that they had done a good job and we were ready to move into the finished 1/3 section of our house. Mike Barnett loaned us a temporary fence for our dogs for underneath the house, while we were on his waiting list to fence the entire yard.

The first of February, we finally moved into the finished part of our house. It is still in a serious "ICU state", but at least now, we all had personal space. The first night in the house, we all, (pups included), took our own little private corners. The moment was comical; our dogs had even had too much closeness over the past 5+ months!

By the end of February, we had completely cleaned out the middle section of the store. It was such a beautiful sight, being able see the entire concrete floor! The debris and mud were all gone! We told our sales rep's to start sending us merchandise, we were re-opening! We had built a wall to block the totally destroyed section, re-insulated and had the other walls put up. We opened up 1/3 of the store on March 15th for the start of the season, Spring Break! Then, on May 19th, we demolished the collapsed section, in a matter of hours! On July 10th, we finished rebuilding the next phase and opened it back up. Now, somewhat of all evidence of the destruction is going away!

An additional positive moment, when the Crenshaw Elementary school re-opened in February, I got a pleasant surprise from Cindy Rodriguez. She found my purse in her locked office in a white trash bag, tied up with duct tape and a message on a paper towel written by Al and Mary. They had saved my purse and all was secured and safe inside!

So we continue through our lives still repairing from IKE; knowing we can work so, so hard to get what we have and it can still disappear from us within a blink!! Throughout the years, one of my dad's favorite sayings, "Rome wasn't built in a day!"… But we now know that "ROME *can* be destroyed in a day!!" We have learned more than we ever wanted to know about life within a one year time frame!! We take life for granted and life is not granted to us. Life is so very precious and within a day, our life and the life we create can quickly disappear from us. We have learned that the most important thing about life is all of us together. We all are the ones that make life worthwhile….the love, the community, the family and the friends….together!!...and with GOD!!

GENE AND JEAN STRAATMEYER

"When I look at your heavens, the work of your fingers, the moon and the stars that you have established, what are human beings that you are mindful of them, mortal that you care for them?" Psalm 8: 3-4

IKE - ON THE FIRST ANNIVERSARY AFTERWARDS

This "First anniversary of IKE" memoir deals first with our community's recovery and secondly with our life as we experienced the storm and our personal recovery efforts. IKE blew through our Peninsula in the early morning hours of September 13, 2008 and created devastation we have never seen in our three score and more years. It was the third most destructive hurricane to hit the U.S. We survived IKE and we have worked diligently to rebuild our own lives and the well-being of our community.

The damaged and recovering Peninsula

Our first thought when we came back to the Peninsula was, "What will be done to clean up this horrendous mess?" Sand covered everything including roads and driveways. Three thousand five hundred homes were gone while more than a thousand others were savagely ripped so wide open that blue tarps couldn't cover the gaps. Some of the dismantled homes floated board by board north across Galveston Bay and their debris ended up on a distant shoreline in Chambers County. It was burned there because there was no way to remove it - marshland, alligators, and snakes all defended their newly acquired stockpile of lumber. The rest of the debris was spread across the Peninsula. Think of the insides of 5,000 homes being belched out by a 120 mile per hour wind. The aftermath resulted in thousands of semi loads of debris being hauled off to distant "dumps," as we called them where I grew up.

The miracle is that the removal was done with an environmental touch. Debris was hauled to an open field near our home and then it was separated as it was being unloaded. Refrigerators, air conditioners, washing machines, televisions, computers, cars and the like were placed in separate areas. Wood landed in one pile while wrecked cars were placed in another! Anything remaining was put into yet another pile and then semi trucks hauled each pile to different areas off the Peninsula. It took at least eight months before we saw a cleaned-up community looking like it was naked. Most of the trees, lawns and roads were gone. After the debris was out, only scattered houses were left - awkwardly sticking upward in the sand here and there, making the Peninsula look barren and beaten.

As debris removal was taking place, the building and rebuilding process began. This meant work and it didn't take long before workers started pouring onto the Peninsula. They came to build new homes, rebuild damaged ones and to help get entrepreneurs back in business. I saw license plates from as far away as Oregon and Indiana and as nearby as Louisiana.

This influx of "storm chasers" quickly inflated the Peninsula's trailer population. Pre-IKE trailer parks filled up overnight and new ones sprang into being from one end of the Peninsula to the other. Construction workers poured in, pulling travel trailers behind their trucks. In addition, a FEMA trailer park opened in High Island and it had the amenities of paved streets and house numbers on every trailer. FEMA trailers also popped up in Crystal Beach, not in a FEMA trailer park, but on individual cement slabs where the owner lost his or her home. It is my understanding that these trailers were a FEMA "mistake" because it is against FEMA regulations to place their trailers in a flood plain, and the whole Peninsula is a flood plain except for High Island. However, once placed, the FEMA trailers remain for now.

One or two people "hoodwinked" FEMA. They owned homes in distant cities but convinced FEMA their home on the Peninsula was their permanent residence. However, it wasn't and getting a FEMA trailer on their property meant they could come down to the beach for weekends just like they did when their beach house was still standing. I called FEMA about one of them.

Adding to the trailer population were people who lived here and lost their homes to IKE. They pulled trailers onto their storm - cleared lots. Our son, Mike was one of those. He only had to have a permit that his sewer was working; he had to get electricity to his lot; and then hook up. Some overly optimistic residents think this might be the way to go for the future because if another hurricane heads for our shores, they can pull the trailers to safety. However, most of the newer subdivisions won't allow the parked trailers after a two year grace period during which the trailer dwellers must rebuild their homes.

With all the work, a lot of illegal's poured in. Although most contractors dealt with them fairly, a few didn't. I have heard many stories about some illegal's who were scammed. After agreeing they would be paid only when job was finished, the contractor told them to show up the following morning for their wages. When the illegal's arrived the next day, the contractor didn't. He disappeared into the vastness of Texas. What could they do? They couldn't go to the police! These illegals were some of those who needed free food to survive. Other problems developed. Having nowhere to spend the night, the illegals were sometimes caught sleeping in derelict homes, in tents, cars and occasionally on the beach.

I have been asked why I didn't turn them into the authorities and my response if that I would have if the authorities arrested those who employed them. Having lived on the Peninsula for five years and seeing many illegal's working for low wages even before IKE, I believe the Gulf will have ice on it before the employers are arrested.

There was one other problem the community had to face. They were the contractors who came like wise men from afar conning people about what they could do if they were hired. They had smooth tongues and good looking machinery. They had fake business licenses and possessed the mannerisms of decent folks. They persuaded a few of the gullible to give them huge amounts of money in advance and then as the money was transferred to their hands, they immediately vanished into the darkness of the night, never to be seen or heard of again. We know two families who lost $30,000 and $70,000 respectively to these crooks. IKE not only hit our friends with wind and water but with humanity's backwash, people who have no conscience and prey upon those already down and out!

During this first burst of rebuilding and remodeling, the homes were mostly the homes of those who had a settlement from their insurance company or who could afford to rebuild without any financial help from others. Garages had to be replaced, decks had to be rebuilt, houses had to be painted, roofs had to be replaced, roads had to be re-graded and paved, electric lines had to be rebuilt, water lines had to be repaired, sewers had to be rebuilt, sod had to be laid for lawns and permits had to be sought from the County to rebuild anything.

A goodly number of the new homes being built are pre-fabricated and trucked in from elsewhere. This is instant gratification at its peak. Beach house gone after IKE, new home on the beach not much later! However, I am hearing good reports about them, but we won't be certain until they have been tested by the winds and waves of a future hurricane.

The spiritual impact of IKE upon the area is not yet known, I believe. All churches were inoperable after IKE except for those in High Island. In Gilchrist; the Pentecostal, the Baptist and the Full Gospel, were destroyed and floated north to the vast shores of Galveston Bay. For the foreseeable future, I don't see new churches in Gilchrist because IKE took 598 - 600 homes in the community and there aren't enough residents back for the resources needed to build a new church and maintain a congregation.

In Crystal Beach, the Church of Christ and the Roman Catholic Church were "raptured" to church heaven while the Methodists and Baptists were only decommissioned for worship. Both had severe building damage. The Church of Christ is now meeting in a donated Upper Room, (building on pilings), while the Methodists and Baptists have returned to worship in parts of their buildings. The Men's Prayer Breakfast at the Methodist Church is back in business. The Roman Catholics are "massing" in the school.

I am not sure about Sunday attendance at the churches since so many who were homeless after the hurricane moved away. However, in the aftermath of IKE I can say that the churches are not seeing more of the non-churched in their make-do sanctuaries. This could be due to the strange mixture of culture and religion here that includes strong doses of civil religion. Civil religion, in my opinion, mitigates the distinct line between culture and religion. Those who don't worship regularly seem to have a fluent religious vocabulary and for them religion and community are intertwined. It seems to me that worship is not that important when prayer is included before public meetings and even football games. With civil religion intertwined with secular life, the community is not anti-religious. Just the opposite - it is very pro evangelical Christianity. I haven't heard anyone in the community say they wish the churches would not rebuild. Rather, they all rejoice when the churches become sanctuaried and functional once more even though they themselves will not be a supporter of or a regular worshiper in them. I have never lived in a community before where culture and religion are so entwined with the result being that spirituality is present everywhere but it is not vibrant.

In Port Bolivar, the Baptist church and the Roman Catholic Church were both de-commissioned by IKE. The Baptists are repairing their building while Roman Catholic laity is arguing, unsuccessfully, I think, with the Cardinal in Galveston. The congregants think the church is repairable and feel such an historic church should be the recipient of saving grace. But the Cardinal's judgment seems to be final and he promises that one, new, more hurricane-proof church will be constructed in the Crystal Beach area to serve the Roman Catholics on the Peninsula.

The businesses are slowly coming back. The early ones were makeshift. A travel trailer became a grocery store. Several small trailers became cafes, using picnic tables in front for customer seating. Finally, the Big Store returned with limited groceries and hardware. Now it is slowly growing back to the size it used to be. Our Physician's Assistant returned, remodeling an older home that had been partially destroyed by IKE. The Pharmacy is relocating at ground level below his office. The Post Office was one of the last to come back. There are now three gas stations compared to four before the storm. The bank and a hair stylist have re-located to the Big Store even though the bank will eventually rebuild across the street.

Dannay's Donuts, a popular place on weekends, has returned with a new store. Three cafes which seat people indoors have returned. The lawn-mowing crews have reappeared, and the liquor stores and bars are back in numbers. The illegal gambling establishment's parking lot has more cars in it all the time as the sheriff's patrol cars pass by looking the other way. From what I read locally, several persons say it seems to be easier for law enforcement to give traffic tickets than to deal with what the public considers more important crimes. Some in the community appreciate the illegal gambling because they want gambling legalized here and in the State. They continued to argue that gambling will fuel an economic recovery for the Peninsula and Galveston and that we need to keep the money in Texas instead of sending it to the American Gambling Casinos in Louisiana.

Saturday, September 13, 2009 the community celebrated the first anniversary of IKE with a full house at the local school gym. Ten Peninsula residents who died in the storm were remembered as well as the four who are still missing. Bodies are still being found - one just this past week across Galveston Bay buried under debris. The skeletal remains are being identified as I type.

The celebration was one of remembrance and planting hope for the future. No one knows how long it will be before the community can say we will be totally back. A neighbor of mine who has lived here nigh on forever and operated a business before IKE, told me this morning that he feels it will take years for the vacant lots to be filled with homes again - and some never will, because the State is buying many of the lots that once had homes on them. It seems like the long term direction of the State over the next century is to start buying lots now that once had homes on them and when future hurricanes come they will continue the buy out until they can eventually make the entire Peninsula into a wild life refuge - parts of it already are. It really isn't a bad idea except for those who have lived on the Peninsula since the Indians were chased away. They don't like it. They have deep roots including families that have always called this peninsula home. And, I think the buyout by the state may end up having the Peninsula look strange with a vacant lot here and a vacant lot there. I wonder who is going to mow the grass or chop the weeds on all that vacant property?

For the future, County government and the State of Texas are talking about an IKE DIKE - patterned after those in the Netherlands and Northwestern Germany where the dikes protect the residents from the vicious storms of the North Sea. In fact, before those dikes were built, my ancestors, who resided in Northwest Germany, inhabited small houses elevated on poles so that when the sea came inland on the winds of a storm, they were safe and dry.

Galveston was saved by a sea wall - the surge was defused when it hit the 12 feet high cement barrier and most of the damage in Galveston was due to flooding - from the water which did an end run around the sea wall and entered Galveston from the Bay.

The Ike Dike probably won't happen because of the cost. We live in a different time from when the sea wall was built after the 1900 hurricane which took some 6-8000 lives. Afterwards, the city rebuilt without government help and built the sea wall without FEMA Funds. Maybe they were of a hardier stock than we are today. For the present, it was just announced, that the State of Texas and Galveston County will rebuild the dunes that IKE's water washed over the Peninsula.

There is some new government money coming soon for middle class and poor folks, who lost their homes. It will amount to millions of dollars - and for a year or two another building booms will occur. Until it comes, progress will be slower.

PERSONAL REMEMBRANCES AND REFLECTIONS OF IKE

- THE REV. DR. GENE STRAATMEYER

We left a day and a half before IKE officially hit the Peninsula. Our son, Mike helped us nail the plywood to the front windows. We had previously put hurricane blinds on the back. Mike's house already had them so he buttoned up quickly. Earlier in the morning we pulled his "vintage" 1972 Ford pickup to a friend's house in High Island where it survived the storm without damage. Everything else was left in our ground level garage. Our golf cart and lawn tractor were the biggest items but it also contained everything one has in a storage shed.

We left Crystal beach about 2:00 P.M. on Thursday afternoon with a stiff wind already blowing off the ocean. The Ferry was shutting down at sunset and since we believed there would be a long line, we headed northeast to High Island. There is a low bridge at Rollover Pass where the Peninsula is only a quarter mile wide. When we crossed, the ocean waves were already high enough so that the water sprayed over the highway.

Our son-in-law stayed back to complete a few finishing touches on our daughter Sandee's house and in the process fell off a high ladder and landed on the cement driveway. Neighbors still there called the ambulance and fortunately a few of the fire department volunteers were still around so he was taken by ambulance to Galveston. They held the Ferry and he went straight across to the University of Texas Medical Branch in Galveston. Although he was hurt, it was not serious, and by evening our grandsons had to drive to Galveston to bring him home because the water was rising on Galveston Island and the hospital was being evacuated.

Other residents decided, because it was judged only a Category II Hurricane, to stay on the Peninsula until Friday. But in the early AM hours of Friday, the water was rising rapidly and covering the highway, the only escape route other than by boat. Those who waited until sun-up Friday morning didn't make it because of deep water over the road going to High Island and the ferry was already closed down. Many lived to tell of their brush with death. Some were plucked off the tops of trucks, cars and houses by helicopter Friday afternoon. Saturday afternoon, after a fear filled night and early morning, some were awaiting rescue on their roofs, while some floated across the Bay to Smith Point by hanging on to debris while others were drowned when their homes were swept away by the tidal surge. Pets had to be left behind because the Coast Guard was only rescuing people. One man with an adult tiger and lion took them to the Baptist Church where they weathered the storm. Eleven people who lived on Bolivar Peninsula were killed while three are still missing.

In Sugar Land on Friday morning, we were getting a generator ready, (in case we lost electricity), and purchasing essentials like drinking water and food. IKE hit the Houston area late Friday night and Saturday morning with high winds, several tornadoes and heavy thunderstorms. Because of thousands of fallen trees the electricity went out and for the next several weeks we lived with a generator supplying power for the refrigerator, a lamp or two, television and occasionally computers - but not air conditioning. Our grandkids didn't think they could exist without their modern gadgets but they did. However, they shouted loud "harrahs" when the electricity came back several weeks later.

We anxiously watched television and the computer to search for our homes when there were picture-taking flyovers of the Peninsula. It took a couple of weeks before we learned from television that Gilchrist and Crystal Beach had taken the brunt of IKE, we were told that at one time water covered the whole Peninsula, that the sustained winds had been as high as 110 miles per hour and that the tidal surge had been as high as 18 feet. Over time we came to realize that both Mike and Sandee's houses were gone but that ours was still standing although we didn't know what the damage might be. We assumed the garage and everything in it was gone.

On September 26th we were allowed back to the Peninsula for the first time. It took that long because the highway was covered with three or more feet of sand, houses had floated to the middle of the road and had to be bulldozed to the side, a part of the bridge over Rollover Pass was out and there were no services like grocery stores, gas stations, post office, water, cafes and electricity.

We woke up early that morning and drove from Sugar Land to Winnie and then south to High Island. No one was allowed in until sunrise since looting had become a problem. No one was allowed to be on the Peninsula if they didn't have proof of residency. We had an old electric bill with our name and post office box on it. We encountered a mile long line of cars at 6:00 A.M. about six miles north of High Island so we waited in the dark until the first rays of light appeared on the eastern horizon. Then we were cleared and drove the 20 miles through High Island to our house in the Sand Castle subdivision.

As we pulled up, the driveway was covered with drifts of sand at least three feet high. A slimy mud covered the garage floor. Everything under the garage was gone, the walls, the golf cart, the lawnmower, the tools - there was nothing but vacant space and a lot of debris from houses in front of us that didn't make it past our downstairs. Our pillars were scarred from parts of other houses washing under ours. Seven houses between our house and the beach were gone. Where we once had only a small view of the Gulf of Mexico, now there was a vast expanse of ocean visible from our deck.

Even our stairs were still there, so we climbed to the deck, tore off the plywood and unlocked the door. Inside it was just as we left it weeks before.

There was no damage to speak of except some things fell off a shelf. With winds of 110 miles per hour and gusts that may have been higher, our relatively new home must have shaken, rattled and rolled - but it refused to kneel and humble itself before IKE. Even the shingles held on.

Our first thought was what this meant. Most neighbors and fellow residents on the Peninsula lost everything. Most people ask "Why me Lord?" when they face tragedy and there were many on this sand bar that asked that very question. However, we asked, "Why us Lord?" Why were we spared and others weren't? I think it is a common response in times of disaster - some are almost unscathed while others are scared, battered and even lose their life. Survivors wonder why they came through the devastation unscathed. What is God trying to communicate?

We also gave thanks to God for sparing our home and prayed for those who arrived at their homes to see nothing but a cement slab or a battered, unlivable house. If everyone had come back to the Peninsula at the same time, I believe all the debris and all the sand would have been wet with tears. This was a staggering loss for so many residents who lived here and owned homes here.

Before IKE there were 6,500 homes on the Peninsula. Only 3% were in the kind of shape where residents could move back in immediately. Another 3,500 were totally blown or washed away. Most of the rest were in such bad shape that in the days ahead they kept carpenters occupied for a long time.

A week or so later we moved back even though we had no electricity, no sewer and no water. Groceries and mail pickup were 35 miles away, gasoline 14 miles away and the Ferry was only hauling work crews and equipment across from Galveston.

Having grown up in rural South Dakota during the Great Depression and World War II, we knew what it was like not to have all the conveniences so "making the best of the situation" wasn't as hard as it might seem. There were many who thought IKE had affected our brains - they couldn't live without conveniences and believed that those who did needed a psychologist. Consequently, most residents who had homes that were livable didn't get back until Christmas. In addition, having lived 21 years in Alaska where we became campers, made another big difference. It helped us survive more comfortably.

During our first month on the Peninsula, it was very dark at night and that made the stars brighter than I had seen them since I was a boy living on a farm in South Dakota without electricity. Jean and I often sat on the deck and listened to the silence and ogled at the marvelous universe above us. What we saw reminded me of the Psalmist (8:3-4) who said, "When I look at your heavens, the work of your fingers, the moon and the stars that you have established; what are human beings that you are mindful of them, mortal that you care for them?" Comparing what was above us and the absolute chaos around us made for many thoughts about God's providence and God's relationship to suffering. IKE caused great emotional damage to people here, some of those who stayed were injured and death to others who didn't make it out.

Martial law had been declared so cars or people couldn't enter the Peninsula before sunrise and they had to be out by sunset. Even when we drove to Winnie for groceries and mail, we had to make certain we were back before twilight or we would not be let in until the following morning. When we were home at night, we were not allowed to step away from our house. Anyone found outside of a building was arrested because looting was still a problem and police and National Guard were patrolling the area. After all the workers left between 5-6 P.M., silence descended on the landscape and stayed until sunrise. About all we heard was the occasional distant splash of a wave hitting the beach, an occasional, distant gunshot and the National Guard ATV's which they used to get around because roads were not passable.

But, life moves forward and we had to get ourselves back to normal. Thank God for our son, Mike. He has a John Deere tractor with a front end loader and he removed the sand from the driveway and the rest of the lot. He prepared the electricity for hook up. We have a complicated individual home sewer system and it took a specialist and $3,500 to get it working again after the storm surge which washed off the cover and filled it with sand. Our water company worked hard and running water came back sooner than expected. Mike rebuilt our garage. Our electric company brought in people from all over the country since they had to build 35 miles of new power lines. By Thanksgiving, we were living better but still had no sewer. The family who gathered at our house had to go outdoors to a port-a-potty. The grandkids had a hard time with that. But by Christmas we no longer had to haul water and gas from High Island, although we still had to get groceries and mail from Winnie. Electricity, water and television were back just before New Years. Thank God for cell phones. We were never out of communication with family and friends. Snail mail was the last of the conveniences that returned.

About a month after the new construction was finished below the house, we had our house totally repainted. Any day now, we will have our deck resealed and then one last task remains - to re-sod the lawn. Then we will be back to where we were a year ago.

Son Mike bought a fifth wheel trailer and pulled it on his lot. As a carpenter, he has had plenty of work restoring IKE damaged homes and rebuilding new ones. He is drawing plans for his new home so he can rebuild. Daughter Sandee hasn't decided whether to rebuild or not. Without the grandchildren being here almost every weekend as they were before IKE, our life has changed. We spend a lot less time on the beach and there are fewer family gatherings.

As we look back on the year, we see that it was an emotional rollercoaster. We left our home with local historical information that ocean water had never, in the recollection of those who lived here for many years, gotten over the sand dunes on the beach. We also heard television and radio reports that it was going to veer away from us. What we expected was only high winds, and that isn't what happened. Besides the wind there was towering wall of water that destroyed almost everything in its path.

Once we were back living on the Peninsula, we found community needs staring directly in our face. And our response was affirmative. After all, IKE didn't destroy our Christian faith and a large part of our faith is servant hood. There were so few of us living here at the outset and someone had to put their hand on the plow.

I was Vice President of the Bolivar Peninsula Community Outreach (BPCO) before IKE. The president lost his him home, decided not to rebuild and moved away. That automatically put me into a leadership position.

The first task was bringing potable water and food for the residents and workers. Before we finished this project, in cooperation with Volunteer Organizations Active in Disasters (VOAD), 44 semi-loads of water were delivered and 14 semis of Meals Ready to Eat (MRE).

Hearing of $2,000,000.00 (two million) in private gifts given to restore homes in Galveston County, I immediately set up an ad hoc committee of BPCO to get Bolivar Peninsula included. There were many stipulations to getting the money and the very first was having a caseworker. My wife, Jean, with her social work background, volunteered, and for the next two months we were off every Monday to get trained, she for the casework and for me, managing the rebuilding of homes that were funded by the group. The caseworker job was far greater than we imagined, and by the end of August we were about burned out. Jean's responsibility was greater than mine; she had people calling her at all hours and with our home being the office, clients occupied our kitchen table often past the dinner hour.

My responsibility was to recruit volunteers to help rebuild and once they were here to keep them occupied with meaningful work. On September 1, 2009 Jean was relieved of her responsibility when Catholic Charities hired two caseworkers and placed them in an office in Crystal Beach. However, there is a third desk in their office - one for Jean who has become an old pro at enabling the restoration and rebuilding of homes.

Right in the middle of everything we had our biggest emotional blow. Our great, African dog, Malawi died in February. Before IKE he had the deck, the cool downstairs beside the garage and a small part of the grassy backyard. IKE ruined that space. One day Malawi escaped the temporary gate on the deck and wondered to the highway where a fast-moving debris truck hit and killed him instantly. Many tears were shed. We still miss him. He is one of the best dogs we have ever had. A friend had a tombstone made for him that says, "Malawi, if tears could build a stairway and memories a lane, I'd walk right up to doggie heaven and bring you home again." In the midst of all of this Jean finished her third book about this special dog, "An African Dog in Texas." On the first two books, Malawi helped send $8,000 to the orphans of Malawi. Soon, he will send thousands of dollars more to them when his final book is sold.

My responsibility with hurricane recovery has not gone away, but Jean is picking up part of my load.

Part of the stress we felt and still feel are so much need and so little we can do. And the people are stressed as well. Some are arguing with insurance companies. Others are trying to prove ownership of their house or land when everything was washed away. Having a safety deposit box in the local bank didn't help because the whole bank was deposited (no pun intended) into Galveston Bay.

On my end, the frustration was that this Hurricane generated so little help. Money didn't come in as it did with Katrina to assist the survivors. Volunteer numbers were way down. It didn't take very long before we quit advertising the money available from GCR2 because we had people coming to Jean just by word of mouth than she could handle. And, if Jean completed their casework and they were eligible for volunteer help, there were not enough of them to go around. Volunteers are so important because they stretch the available money and thus allow many more to get their homes back to livability.

So as we enter the second year after IKE, we are still involved. We aren't quite sure what the second year after IKE will bring.

ALAN AND KIMBERLY VOIGT

"It's not the destination...it's the journey!"

At the age of 45, who would have thought of writing a story about Hurricane Ike? Living in Crystal Beach all of my life, it has been a fun and unique place to live. My grandparents, Lilly and Joe Rohacek, Sr., had their own concrete business, and they went through Hurricane Carla in September of 1961. I remember their stories of evacuating to Fort Travis with many others. My grandfather had a "gas" water pump to pump the water out. If they had not been able to pump the water out, they would have drowned!

Now, all is gone!! A lot of changes have come to the beach. A lot of people are gone or they have moved off and will never come back. I look at my parents home in Crystal Beach, the trees are all gone, no grass...just an unfamiliar place that was once our home. All of the pine trees and a beautiful Magnolia tree; it would produce beautiful flowers even with all the salt in the air. The tree was one right out of the movie "Gone with the Wind," it will never be replaced.

As I was getting ready to pack up and leave for higher ground I had to put the memories on the back burner. Alan, my Husband, a weather bug kept saying, "We need to get ready to leave." I went to work at Latitude Surf Shop that Wednesday and I also had the owner's four dogs that I was "pet sitting" for. Additionally, I had my own dog, cats and Leroy, my hermit crab. I went to work Wednesday, a quiet sunny day. All of Crystal Beach was quite normal, in a sense! I got off at 5 P.M. and I went to feed the owners dogs and to make sure all was okay. Meantime, I kept calling the owner of the store and updating her about the Hurricane warnings. I went home and Alan had finished boarding up and I told our daughter to pack all of her belongings. I cleaned out the refrigerator and washed all of the dishes…of course, Alan questions, "Why are you washing the dishes?" I then, got my things ready to leave on Thursday. I told Alan that I would not go until I knew that the owners were back to rescue the dogs…he said, "We might not have time to get out!"….I said, "Oh-well, a chance I have to take!"…. "I will take their dogs with us if I have to." The owners drove straight through the night and they were crossing the Texas State Line when I last talked to them on Thursday morning. So now, I was relieved that all was in good hands. Meantime, Alan had gotten up around 6:30 A.M., he woke me up at 7 A.M., He said, "We need to get across Rollover!" I got our daughter up and Alan packed the car and the truck. One of the last things I recall before leaving our neighborhood was Susan, my neighbor! She was struggling with her garage door to get it open to get the generator out. She said "I am staying with my dad!" Herman Shaver is her dad, an old-timer, who refused to leave.

We got the pets all loaded and as we drove away from our home, I prayed, "All would be here when we got back." We did pass the owners of dogs in Gilchrist as we were leaving, at that time, not knowing what a journey they would go through. We drove to my parent's home in Buna, for the duration of the storm. Upon arrival, we got the news of my brother, Robert Reed. It had come to "light" a realization that he was still in Crystal Beach, at the Baptist Church with some friends and with a "real" Lion. He ended up stranded in Crystal Beach trying to help some of his friends. We finally heard from him on Saturday, after the storm. He had been helicopter off the Peninsula and was safe in the San Antonio area. He did manage to come out fine after that ordeal, but what a story he had to tell!!

On September 26th, we were allowed to come back to the Peninsula. We found our home still intact, with 1 1/2 feet of water, mud and just a big mess; there were all kind of parts of the neighbor's houses in our yard. We left the house as is and moved on; we have our lives, some sanity and all will be okay. The tears still come down when I see all of the loss and all of the changes of a place once called home. I now live in Winnie, but still work in Crystal Beach and I still have the "Sand under my feet." Crystal Beach will always be my "home" in my heart!!!

ROBIN HUBER

"Those who sow in tears shall reap in joy." Psalms 126:5

I am the Pastor of the Full Gospel Lighthouse Church, (FGLC), in Gilchrist, Texas. My family and I moved to Gilchrist in November of 1983. My girls, Marie and Racheal attended High Island School. My husband, Al, was the Pastor of FGLC until 2003. He passed away in the back of the church of a massive heart attack. The church asked me to stay, I was there faithfully, until IKE hit! However, I am still coming back every Sunday and I hold church from 12:00 – 2:30 P.M.

The beach was in our blood, it was our home! It was all about the beautiful sunrises and sunsets, and people whom you call friends. Every September, all of the locals in Gilchrist would sit on their decks watching the last of the tourist season end and once again the beach was all ours! So many good memories!

I remarried in 2005 to David Starnes, we continued the work at the church, working steadily with the youth, there was not much for them to do on the beach, so we had an awesome youth night service every Wednesday night… How I miss that to this date!

As we all heard about IKE, not a person on the beach knew it was coming to our town! If we would have known, I know many of us would have packed up U-hauls! My family had stayed several times during a Class 1 and Class 2 hurricanes in the past. No one was expecting what was about to take place!!

As we were preparing to board up the church and home, cleaning the yard up, bringing items into the garage that could fly away…which took all day!! Wednesday evening came quickly and we were tired, so we were thinking about staying that night and leaving out early the next morning. Governor Rick Perry came on the T.V. and announced how bad the storm surge would be if it came into the Gulf. I really did not want to leave. We were waiting still for the "turn" that the IKE was supposed to make. David came into the kitchen of the church and insisted that I should go to my mothers. He knew I would not leave the church, so he made me pack a couple of things and we did leave around 8:00 P.M. that evening. I am telling you, if David would not have come in and insisted on me leaving; I would not be here on this planet today! Thank you David! We drove down to Rollover Pass to look at the water and we saw how high it was and how dangerous it looked! Well really, "angry," is the word on how it looked! We drove to High Island and left my Tahoe at Joe Faggard's home and we took the little black car. We did not know what to expect with the traffic, since we exited for Hurricane Rita several years earlier, which was a nightmare! We did not know if there were lines of traffic on I-10? So as we are on the road, we reach Houston and at that time my daughter, Marie, calls on my mobile and says, "Mom, IKE made the turn, it is headed to Gilchrist!"….I said, "No, way?" As we reached Caldwell late that night, we were exhausted and went to bed! The next morning in Caldwell, we began to feel the winds of IKE; we are about 4 hours away from the coast!! By night, the lights went off and now we are without lights for several days, the only news I could get was from my daughters calling me and letting me hear the news over the phone.

I was so shocked to hear that Gilchrist was GONE…I could not believe it!? I was thinking, maybe flooded really bad…I had no idea that 19 feet of water was there and no town! All I wanted to do was to go home and see my church and my home! When the lights came back on, all we could hear and see on the television was that we were not allowed back home! No pictures were being taken; they would not allow even the news media in!!…What was going on? We all wanted to know! Finally, the news media fought their way in and we saw pictures, no one could believe it!!

I needed to pick up my Tahoe from High Island, so I told my daughters that I wanted to go. Brent, my son-in-law had a 4 wheel drive so we all packed into it and headed to the beach. The State Highway patrols were blocking the roads and you had to have proper I.D., when they saw my I.D. they asked if I wanted to see my property. I said, "You are kidding me right?"....they said, "No, you can look." No one else was there, but they allowed me in...there was no Highway 87; we had to make our own road. We all had our cameras and could not believe what we saw!! We could not even recognize the place; it looked like a bomb blew up the beach!! Cars and trucks in the fields, not knowing if people were still in them dead or alive...Cows dead all along the way...then a few live cows in a daze! How did they survive we asked ourselves? There were dead alligators, furniture and debris all over the place.... "Where was I?" In a war zone?? It took forever to reach Gilchrist, now to try to find the church and my home. You could not recognize anything. Finally, I saw a red house that was on the bay still standing, a land mark now; my property was in front of it. I remember getting out of the truck and just falling on the ground crying...my daughters were crying!! IT WAS HORRIBLE!!

Nothing was left, but a few pilings, and church equipment thrown everywhere. There are no words that can describe how your heart just broke; all you could do is walk around in a daze and cry!

Then Art Rascon from Channel 13 News came up and wanted an interview. We had become friends earlier during the storm; he and Wayne Delcifino were the only 2 people that fought for us to see Gilchrist!! We all can never thank them enough!!! After the interview, the girls and I looked around for anything we could find that was ours. After several hours, we left with just a few items from our church and from our home. To be honest...I never wanted to go back...it was too hard! Everything you have ever worked for was gone under the sea or buried in the sand...and the smell was unbelievable!! The next couple of months were so difficult, as a Pastor, I was working with local families and the Laurie Recovery. Many people were calling me asking me if their family member was alive, or if they were dead. The stress was too much, on top of moving from family member to family members home. May I add, my family, really helped me!! I want to thank my mom, Marie, Racheal, Ron, Brent and Scott. What a wonderful family I have!!! My cousin, Scott Hughes, knew I was beyond stress and offered me his lake home…what a blessing!!! Being homeless was not fun; The stress caught up with me one night and I fainted in the hall of the lake home. When I came to, I had no idea where I was, all I knew was that my teeth were broken and my head was hurting. I had fallen face forward onto a hardwood floor. I had to get myself back to Houston so I could be with my daughters; I was so afraid! I was checked out and I was okay. I came back to the Lake several days later and tried again to start a new life… crying most of the time. I was missing my church and my home.

Now, 1 year later, I am still here at the Lake. I return to the beach every Sunday to hold services from 12 – 2:30 P.M. either in a tent on the church property or in a home in Bolivar. So many people reached out to help me in my time of need….Mike, Dee, Delisa, Paul, Poppy, Joan and the Congregation of Fullness of Christ Church in Dallas…they will never know how they gave me hope!! Hope to go on and the Hope not to give up!! The Bible says in Proverbs 13:1 "Hope deferred makes the heart sick."….We all need HOPE!!!

Winston Churchill gave a commence speech to a college group. He rose to go to the podium and said, "NEVER GIVE UP!" He sat back down. He rose again and said, "NEVER GIVE UP!" He sat back down; He did this the third and a fourth time. NEVER GIVE UP…Were all the words he spoke. That class said they would never forget this speech.

"NEVER GIVE UP!"….Trust GOD, He will see you through. This is the "HOPE" that I leave you with!

LOUISE MELILLI

"Mama Teresa's Flying Pizza and Italian Restaurant"

The restaurant crumbled, yet the sign remained standing.

Our restaurant, Mama Teresa's Flying Pizza and Italian Restaurant was located at 2770 Highway 87 in Crystal Beach. The history of it, basically, it all got its start on a "whim." It was the 20th wedding anniversary of Salvatore and Theresa Melilli, (Mama Teresa herself,) that was the beginning of this "whim." They were driving from their home in New York to Florida and then decided to drive to Texas to visit relatives in Galveston. It was on the long, scenic drive down Highway 87 from Sabine Pass to Port Bolivar that they spotted a for sale sign on this piece of land. It was six years later; Sal built with his own hands the restaurant Mama Teresa's. The doors opened in 1983.

This hands-on policy didn't end with Sal building the restaurant, it was a family ran restaurant. One would often enter to find Mama T herself at the register, if she wasn't there she was sitting with customers chatting and visiting. Sal would be in and out of the kitchen with his white towel tucked in the back pocket of his jeans. Carmen, their son could be found behind the pizza counter and Louise, there youngest, waitressing. The Mama Teresa's family didn't end there. Each and every employee that came in contact with us became a family member. There were many weddings and many births celebrated amongst us. We watched one another grow up. Many a times, Sal would be found at one of the back table talking to one of the many young guys that worked there who needed some kind of advice, (a role Carmen took over after Sal passed away.) There was a unity that seemed so automatic, instilling a pride in the restaurant that resulted in the best pizza and Italian food found on the Gulf Coast. Texas Monthly magazine once gave Mama T's the title of "The Pear of the Gulf Coast."

One thing is certain, there were many memories made at "Mama T's," (as the restaurant was affectionately nicknamed.) There are so many memories that will not be forgotten. For those that ever worked there I think there was nothing we enjoyed more than the insanity of a crazy busy holiday weekend. As the insanity began to strike, Carmen would look at everyone and say, "Let's Rock and Roll!!"…and we did, it was awesome. People were everywhere. The phones would go crazy, the kitchen bell going off constantly letting anyone with a free hand know food was ready. There were three pizza men at the counter benching and tossing dough, making the pizzas. The little kids would watch and anxiously wait for the pizza men to throw them a piece of dough to play with at their table. There was a ton of energy radiating in the air. Everyone moved quickly. Those waiting for food were patient for the most part. Why not, they were on beach time! And what a great time it was!

On September 13, 2008 Hurricane IKE struck. Mama Teresa's was reduced to a pile of rubble. It was a heartbreaking sight. Carmen's other restaurant; the American Grill was destroyed as well. Even though the buildings are gone the hearts that made them, what they were, lives on in everyone that walked through the doors. For that we say, heartfelt, "Thank you." and "Grazie."

KATIE COGHLAN

"Bolivar Peninsula Resident since 1982!!"
"I.I.W.I.I."

Hello all of you dudes and dudettes. This is my personal story of my resurrection from the monster, called IKE. IKE took away my world, stole my church, my friends, our houses, our lives, our loves, our hates; everything...*except our faith*. In all of our "heart of hearts" we know that GOD is good, we are the ones that may drift away, not GOD.

On Wednesday night, September 10, 2008, I was at an Eagle's Auxiliary meeting, in talking, I said, "I am going to stay." I had it planned out, water in the bathtub, plenty of water jugs, batteries, generator, candles, crank radio, cat food, canned goods, etc. I was prepared and I was staying!! Well, enough so that the ladies got angry at me, (not a smile on a face), but my mind was made up!

The next day, on Thursday, my friend, Kenny Lane, came over and he helped me cut down some limbs around the house and he helped me do some more stuff to get ready. I asked him, "Do you and Paula want to stay with me?" but he said, "He didn't know what he was doing." That afternoon, I went by my friends, Dee Ann and Frank Sherman to see what they were going to do and if they wanted to stay with me. They weren't home; I guess, luckily for me, they weren't because I probably would have stayed with them during the storm. They had their own "zoo" going on, so second thoughts, I probably wouldn't have wanted to leave my cats and birds behind. Little did I know at that time, that Kenny would have his own adventures in store for him at "Murphy's Island," and Sherman and Dee Ann would have their own death defying story of survival!! I know it was so terrible to leave your animals!! I don't remember her name, right now, but she was a cool lady, an expert shark tooth finder. She liked to sit on the picnic bench at the Tavern. She had a dog she loved dearly named Reba, she lived in Gilchrist...and she wouldn't leave Reba...later, I found out that they both perished in IKE. In the course of that day and night,

I talked to many people, but mainly my family, frantically saying, "LEAVE." I tried to "down play" the storm, as I had been doing for many years. They always tell you to evacuate, but it is never as bad as the news makes it out to be. Later, in the evening, my mom was saying, "Get out or I'm driving down to get you!" However, I wasn't going anywhere, until….About 10:10 P.M., I heard on the television that the ferry was going to quit running at 11:00 P.M. This is when I thought, "Strange, the storm isn't due for two more days? Why would the ferry stop Thursday night at 11:00 P.M.?" Upon doing quick calculations in my mind, I realized there was no way out by Ferry. I wondered if there still was a washout down in Gilchrist and High Island, but such, that wasn't there anymore…or was it. It had never occurred to me to leave by the Ferry. I figured "they… the officials" must know the road is passable, at least until 11:00 P.M. Against my judgment and all I had prepared to do, fear crept in my heart. I called my brother in Houston, and I told him I was on my way. I left my home in Crystal Beach around 11:30 P.M. I had packed some clothes, my cats, my 5 kittens (that I knew could never make it through a storm) and I left!

We kept track of the storm from my brothers. I had phone calls from everybody that I ever knew, calls from everyone that was scattered. I was just trying to keep up with people, as the news rolls in…"Gilchrist is gone!!" It was like, what do you mean "gone?"…I couldn't imagine, (and I still have a hard time with it that Gilchrist is gone…. and all the people.

For the record people, it wasn't Rollover Pass that hindered people…it was the wash-out! Years ago, if that could have been taken care of more people could have gotten out, at least the ones in Crystal Beach and Gilchrist. Poor Bolivar people didn't have a chance once the Ferry closed, 2 days before the storm. I'm sure a lot of folks, felt as I, just wait until Friday morning…but even that was too late…even by 4:00 A.M. it was too late!

Christy and Mandy were calling from Tyler, every year they would make a beach trip to Crystal Beach, to go to Genie's, the Firehouse, The Eagle's, to "Daddy's," Rollover Café, the Wheel, Beach Rock, Sharky's, the Tavern and always a stop at "The Big Store," the zoo, water slide, Fun Town, they would eat at the Outrigger, Decoux's, and Coba's. They stayed at my house, so they knew the area well. Christy and JB, (another friend from Tyler), would make beach trips a few times a year to go fishing at Rollover Pass. They had gotten on the computer and found my subdivision and what they thought was the roof of my house. We weren't for sure, but there was hope it was there. They got in touch with my parents and my parents got in touch with me in Houston. Grant it, as for everyone, communication was extremely poor; everyone was in the streets, homeless and we were all on our cell phones…with very little reception!…It was not comical and comical at the same time, because we were all in, reality, repeating that television commercial… "Can you hear me now?"

Okay, sitting in Houston, at Kelly and Brenda's house glued to the television for any information, Brenda yelled, "Someone from Crystal Beach is talking!"…it was Sherman, saying, "We are trapped and cannot make it to the roof!"…I think he said, "My wife is old!" (I bet Dee Ann is still after Sherman for that comment!) But oh, what a Godsend to hear his voice!! There had been reports that they were dead…I had believed in my heart that they were! Then to watch them being interviewed on television….Oh, I cried so hard out of joy!!!

It is so difficult getting this down, there are so many; too many emotions involved!! I stayed in Houston for a little over a week; I then went to my parents in East Texas. I stayed there until we could come back; I think it was 2 weeks and one day that we had to wait. New problems arised, where to stay? There are no hotels, no vacancies anywhere, even calling to Nacogdoches…no place to stay. I finally found a hotel room out of Houston on the loop. I had a dentist appointment in Fannett; then I was driving to Houston. My friend, Donna Bass, said she lived around where my dentist was and to come by, she said, "In fact, why don't you cancel your room and stay with Nickie, Jerry Wayne and me!" Oh, what a Godsend, that was! Until the day I die, I will always be grateful and indebted to her.

The next morning was the first day they let people back on to Bolivar. Jerry Wayne Fitch drove me…Donna didn't want to see it, yet! We were taking my truck; I had a cat carrier and cat food. Jerry Wayne asked, "What's that for?" I said "just in case any of my porch cats are there." He said, "Baby, I don't mean to hurt your feelings or discourage you, but I seriously doubt you have any cats there!"….but there, again, was hope! Sure enough, my house was there, looked perfect from outside, along with tons of debris, fallen trees, a pontoon boat, a Wells Cargo Wagon, sheds, chairs, pieces of everything and no complete anything. We cleared the steps enough to crawl up them. Everything was muddied and trashed…water came up from under my house about 3 ½ feet. My cockatiels were alive, water had been up to their perches, but they were alive. As Jerry Wayne and I are getting out what we could, he hears a "meow," then I heard it…but we couldn't tell where it was coming from. After "calling" a little face pokes through the bushes, we got the carrier and food and called it up, (not knowing "who" it is.) Then out comes "Woodsy," one of the few porch cats I had named. We kenneled him up….and at that point Jerry Wayne says, "Well baby, maybe there is something to that praying, you do, over your animals!" I responded, "Yes, JW, there is!!" We went back to Donna's with birds, a cat and "stuff." This is not what she bargained for, but she was more than kind to me.

I found my friend, Trish White, in Winnie. Stressed, I needed help getting things out of my house. She had her own world to take care of, but every morning I'd drive in, pick her up early, (I think around 7:00 A.M.), we'd drive to Crystal Beach and work. We tried to figure out, what in the world to do and how do we do it? One day, I was sitting outside my house, in the mud, on a bench. A car passes then backs up. Two men get out, we talk and he told me they had been working in Galveston and they were on their way home. I showed him my downstairs, ceilings ripped down, and everything was muddy! I told him, "I can't figure out how to clear this? I will have to break out the walls to get things cleared." Anyway, he took my name and number and left. Oh, the woman with them gave me a quilt!

I would stay approximately 2 weeks at Donna's, then go to my parents to re-group, drop off things, pick up things, etc. During one of these visits, I received a call from Gerry Lang, saying my name and number had been passed to her. It turns out, those people that stopped, were Menninites and I was fortunate enough to be on their list. They helped clear the downstairs and upstairs. I think it would have been impossible for me without them!! I thank Gerry and the Menninites from Washington, Nebraska and the Dakota's! I will never forget their help to me!!

I was finally eligible for a hotel room in Winnie, which I called home for several months. Trish and I still working on the house…in fact, we still are! In time, it just changes what projects we are doing. I couldn't have made it without Trish's help, support, her friend Henry, her confidence, her faith and "her blood, sweat and tears!"

So far, I have moved from the Quality Inn, to a FEMA trailer in Winnie, to presently the FEMA Park in High Island. While all along, being blessed to have a house to rebuild, back and forth, everyday, from High Island to Crystal Beach!! I, everyday, pass through the sad, poor remains of Gilchrist; the little town that held my church, the Full Gospel Lighthouse Church, my "places of interest"… Rollover Café and Bait Shop, soon to open Lafitte's Hide-away (where the old Genie Bell's on the cut used to be), The Tavern, Ben Bruce's Four Star Quality Bait Camp and store, Claude's Store, Sam's little Sunrise store, the Firehouse (formally the Bolivar Landing and the Corner Cafe.) I constantly think about the days of riding Bill Parker's golf cart with Chris Ribelin Baker, just visiting "everybody." The many times of jumping on the trampoline after a visit to the tavern….laughing, laughing and laughing. How I miss those rides…How I miss that town…and all of the colorful people that made up the town! How I miss our world before IKE…and still, how grateful I am to be here! However, not the same and I never will be! I am grateful to have lived in my paradise for 26+ years. I am grateful to have lived in Gilchrist during the time when Joe Faggard was Constable, Judge Richard Black was our Judge, Byron Wolf had the Trading Post, and Maxis had Tim's Restaurant and Little T's in Crystal Beach (most recently known as Sharky's.) Everything, everyplace and everybody! I am sorry how IKE trashed our world, but I am grateful to have been a part of it! The phone just rang, it was Chris, (I spoke of earlier), she's living in California; she had to take her dad, "Wild Bill Parker," to live there. Their home was on Deen's Road in Gilchrist, she was telling me that she heard their land made it past the Mean High Tide, to where they could build back. I assured her that was true and that, "it is not over yet!" It is still anybody's guess about Rollover Pass, but I'm trying to get some information. It can be hard for local people to get information, much less, if you live out of state, what and how to do it and who to talk to? It has been over a year now, and there are still a lot of people that need help, prayers and advice. But again, that is one of the things which made this such a special community. You don't even have to know them, but there are people to help you and people do help. Well, this is the end of my 1 year story, but hopefully, not the end of my story. I want to thank all that have helped me…and to my brother, his wife, my sweet parents and Jesus Christ! Okay, to all of you dudes and dudettes, this is Katie Coghlan signing off, for now! PEACE!

"I.I.W.I.I., IT IS WHAT IT IS!!"

KATIE COGHLAN

P.S. A special thought of remembrance to a few of my friends of the Bolivar Peninsula. A remembrance to Ben Bruce, Leonard Boone, Vickie Smith, "Pee-Wee", Sandy Walton, Ms. Gracie, and to Billy Baggett "Fish" (whom has been diagnosed with Lou Gehrig's disease,) Midge Parker, Kim Cox, Keith Parker, Estelle and Sloan, Glenda, Beverly, Ju-Ju, Genie Bell, Elaine, Randy Taylor, Moses, Marilyn and Doug Force, Berita, Big Al, Duane Devinn, Steve Sutton, Ingrid, Jessica Williams, Preacher Al, Jimmy Baker, Ron LaForce, Bob Barker, Butch, Herbie, Nootsie, "Sister", Big Steve and little Steve Caracher, Bill Bell, Ms. Rita, "Ru-Ru" Rhonda Hayes, Mr. L.A. French, Charlie Williams, Charlene Keeling, Wendy Pencil, Wendy, Veronica and "Ronnie" Petrie, Mr. Farris, Mr. Tucker, Bad Billy Yellott, Animal, Suzy, Patsy Jones and her sister, Zan Faggard, Buster Merrindinos Momma, Jimmy Lager, Leana, Mark Little, "Gator" Daily, Hilda Bullington, Bicycle Trish, Trish Luquette, Sophia and "Dr. Pepper Jack", Skip, Willie, Sandy (Wick's 4 legged baby), Richard Kelly, Janet Kreuzer, Mary Kahla, Sam Brown, Little Stephanie, Granny Jones, Sandy "Sassy", Paul, Junior, Wells and Loretta Fagg, Gladys Campbell, Mike – the Vike, Shitty Kitty, Nue-Nue, Broke-Neck Jim, Charlie Adams, Glynn Griffin, J.R., H.K., Willie Green, Digger, Calvin Little, Beth Dingler, Alfred "Sweed" Soderman, Jessie Stanley, Robert King, B.J. and Wanda Flannagan, Debbie E. Flannigan, Johnny McDowell, Paw-Paw Pat, Mr. Yancey, Speedy Wilson, Donald Lee Hooks, Big Donna and her husband, Colorado Debbie, Baine Price Leonard Allen Gib Brousard, Robert Land, Lee Standridge, Maggie-Sheila's 4 legged baby, Glenda Gill Jobe and a very colorful fella Ricky Black.

Last but not least to "Lafayett's Hideaway," the newest business in Gilchrist, Texas. It never got to open to the public. Trish White had gone to extremes to remodel the old "Genie's" at the cut. There was a week when locals could come in an experience a Pirate's Cove complete with the atmosphere of pirate maps, et al. There were pool tables, juke boxes, a stainless steel kitchen for small orders. It was going to be a fun place…fun that never got to be. Bad Mama

Jama IKE took it away, except for 2 or 3 of the black irons that were found. Again, don't you wonder where everything went to?

May these names never be forgotten, they were a part of the Bolivar Peninsula and they all had stories, too! The sounds of their laughter faded, as the lights dimmed.

And again, a very grateful thank you to Donna Bass, for opening up your home and your heart to me, to Trish White for helping me at ungodly hours in the mornings, in the mud, slop, trash, blood, sweat and tears and your continual help trying to get my house back in living order. I thank Nancy and Rick for their Tavern Gatherings at the Pass every month. What a wonderful time that is…to visit with old and new faces. Thank you both for helping Gilchrist, Texas, "to come back!" and not be forgotten. I thank my Pastor, Robin Huber Starnes, although our church building is in the bay somewhere, she has continued to drive from Cold Springs for us to have services. I thank my parents for continual uplifting and love to me, and I have been someone that has not been so easy to love for over a year now. I thank "Mr. Man" for having Coconuts, a great place to go that isn't far from my new home. It is a place to get warmed up or cooled off, or "get a lead" on who can move out mud or move in dirt or anything you may need. I especially enjoy it for being the place where I came to learn of the band, "Laurel and The Electric Circus." In a strange way, that group of musicians has given me hope and a new "spark for life." Besides the great music, they have become good friends. Laurel, Jake, Deen, Missy and Tarka, thank you for being in my life. I know many others feel the same and to you Jadeen for hearing the music and watching a high energy performance and saying, "oh my Gosh, She's on the floor."…and of course to "Ci-Ci" who makes it happen. God does work in mysterious ways…and putting Laurel/Missy and "the crew" in my life is one of those ways. Being a member of the Fraternal Order of the Eagles Auxiliary, is one of those ways too. The women, not only from our local organization, but district, State and beyond have proved to be such supporting friends. I have met so many women since IKE that aren't just "Eagle's," but are truly friends and care about how our lives are in the aftermath of IKE…to all of you, thank you, (especially to Oklahoma, Colorado, Orange and Bay City)…you know who you are. A thank you to Maureen for opening her home so we can have our ladies meeting there, until our new area home is erected…hope, hope, hope. I want to thank you God for HOPE. "Hope springs eternal," so I've heard. I don't know what that means, but I do know that hope and faith can get you through a world of woes. "I.I.W.I.I"….It is what it is!!....it is all in how you look at it and what you do with it. You can go down crying or rise up screaming or roll over laughing…or wake up every day with remorse that our beautiful paradise of Bolivar Peninsula and all the beautiful people that made up a special, one of a kind place to live or visit is here no more. Poop on you IKE. You took it away, but you did not kill the spirit. I will not go gently into the good night. I.I.W.I.I… and I do my best to be happy and try to spread cheer in a messed up, muddy, recovering war zone. Thanks again Fred, (Trish's Henry.) Whoever is reading this, I hope it uplifts you, may it somehow bring you hope, spark a memory or make you laugh. Oh, and above all, don't forget to pray! My goodness, I nearly forgot a very, very important thank you. To the one that thought this book up and had an insight to get people involved. At first, my first thought was "No Way," what I feel or have been through or still going through could never be put in words…this writing has been a wonderful therapy. A chance to remember good things, good people, funny unbelievable stories, (that can't be printed!) It has given me a chance to remember the precious and not just feel the peril of doom. I want to thank you, Sarah Standridge and also your husband. The book is cheaper than a therapist. I want to thank you for letting me share my story.

Katie Coghlan

GORDAN AND CHERYL SMALL

"There's no place like home!"

When my husband and I got married on August 16, 2008, we didn't know how our new life together would be. We looked forward to spending our life together in the house we owned. However, little did we know a month later what was ahead of us!

We first heard about Hurricane IKE in the Gulf, we thought it would go somewhere else. We didn't think it would really affect us…personally. We were wrong! We assumed it would be like Hurricane Rita; we would leave for a couple of days, then come back and do repairs.

We worked hard for what we had. I was working at the Big Store as cashier and my husband, is retired. At the store, we were keeping a very close eye on the storm. Night's before it hit, the radar showed it was getting close. So my husband and I sat down and discussed what we should do. He wanted to stay and ride it out, I wanted to leave. We finally decided to leave. I called the supervisor at the store and let her know we were going to go to safety. She agreed and said, "You have to do what you have to do for safety."

I packed a couple of suitcases and what I could for a few days. We loaded up the car. We took his truck and a new lawn mower on a trailer to his cousin's place.

On the morning of September 11, 2008, we headed to Gordon's brother's house in Webster…there we thought would be safe! We stopped by the store to get some things, it was already closed down and they were getting ready to leave. So we headed to the Ferry with others evacuating. As we were on the Ferry, we heard on the radio, that the Webster area was to start evacuating. So we decided to go to his daughter's house in the Austin area.

When we got to his daughter's house, 8 – 9 hours later, we were watching the news when they announced it was coming in over Galveston and the Bolivar Peninsula. The water was rising and people were trapped with no way out! It was a very long night with little sleep. We were waiting for news, when we could come back. We got little or no news about the Bolivar Peninsula the next day. So I sent an e-mailed to Channel 11 News to find out about the Peninsula and our home.

A couple of days later we saw a helicopter do a fly over the damaged areas. We really knew the true reality of the situation we were to face. I saw people we knew on the television that had gotten out saying, "There was no longer a Gilchrist, Crystal Beach or Bolivar…they were no more." Then we saw the flyover. The Peninsula was there, but it was very different. When the helicopter got to Rollover Pass and showed a glimpsed of Gilchrist, I could not believe my eyes. Then I saw a military helicopter turn the news chopper around, before we got a good look and the screen went blank.

I called my boss and asked if he had any word on the impact of the storm. He said, "He didn't know yet, but to keep in touch." So I called one of the police officers I knew, and asked him if he had any word on the impact of the storm. He told me the truth of the situation, it was very grim. He said, "Gilchrist is totally wiped-out, not very much was left." It was a big shock to me!

Then we started hearing about some survivors who rode out the storm and the ones who did not make it. We were finally getting pictures on the internet and on the television of the destruction from the storm. It was hard to see them, but I knew I had to see them so I could get through the shock.

When people were finally able to come back, some friends of ours, got pictures of what we had left, nothing at all, but 4 poles. That was all that was left of our home. We knew we had to make up our minds whether to come back or not.

We stayed with my husband's daughter for a while. We filed a FEMA Claim and we waited. A month later FEMA helped with some money to help us to get back on our feet. We got a travel trailer and things we needed to live on our own. We stayed up there for 4 months, then we decided to come back home. In January, we came back and saw for ourselves what was here. No water, no lights, no nothing…but people trying to get their lives back together.

I cried when I saw the Peninsula, the store and our property for the first time. However, that is when we said we were coming home and rebuild our life here. We couldn't make it up in the Austin area, no matter how hard we tried.

We stayed in Galveston at my brother-in-law's beach house that survived. We came back and forth across the Ferry that was back up and running. We stopped at the store and looked around. I saw my boss and other co-workers working to rebuild and open the store.

Gulf Coast Market/The Big Store

I asked my boss, if I had a job here and he said, "When can you start?" I helped where I could to get the store up and going. I helped clean up our property, while looking around our neighborhood, trying to find something of ours. I found a piano music box that was my mother-in-law's, I got after she died the year before, and some pans and a vase and a few other things we had. It was lost memories we had back. All was not lost! It gave us hope we could make it!!

We finally got a permit for us to put a trailer on our property. We got a bigger trailer and got things set up. We were still coming back and forth from Galveston, but we were home. In late January, we got water, lights, and all the things we needed to live here. We were working on getting our lives back; and the store ready to re-open. We were all starting from the ground up. Our neighbors were slowly starting to come back. We were getting our neighborhood back!

It goes to show, when you think all is lost, there is a light at the end of the dark tunnel! I felt like Dorothy in the "Wizard of Oz", clicking her heels in the ruby slippers saying, "There is no place like home!" This is our home and we are happy to be back here! We made it through the rough times, to stronger better people. Thanks to everyone who worked hard to bring life back to the Bolivar Peninsula.

WE LOVE YOU ALL!!

JACK WINGFIELD

"Southwest of Solitude"

It was April 2007. I had been house hunting for a few months. I looked at houses all over the Southeast Texas area. In February, I had even gone down to the Bolivar Peninsula and looked at a few beach cabins there, as well. One house, out of all of the houses and cabins that I had seen, kept coming back to me. It was in Crystal Beach, an hour from my job. It had a great bar, an awesome deck and had windows all the way around on the beach side. Perfect. One Saturday, I just decided to make the drive there and check it out again. I didn't even have to go in. I called my realtor and said, "I'm ready to make an offer." One month later, I was the newest resident of Crystal Beach.

The place was great! There were two huge Canary Island Date Palms in the front yard. The Gulf of Mexico was my back yard. My cabin was called, "Twin Palms." Cool name, and it fit, but it wasn't MY name. It took me a couple of weeks to come up with the perfect name. I was having a conversation with one of my best friends, Rachael. She said something like, "I bet you're going to be partying like crazy down there." I said, "I didn't buy it to party, I bought it for the Solitude." She said, "You should call it Solitude." I kicked that around a couple of days and one day, driving that way, I looked at the compass on my truck and there it was… "SW." Southwest of Solitude.

I loved the place, it changed my whole life. I had never drank a Corona in my life. I had never grilled anything and I had never really cared for Mexican food. Now all three things are pretty much a way of life for me, even though I don't even live at the beach anymore. When I go gift shopping, I shop at surf shops. I was driving 120 miles round trip every day to work and I didn't care. Not one bit! If I had lived somewhere else, it would have been different.

My place became the "Family get together" place. Of course, it's a beach cabin. We grilled, had some drinks, played guitar and sang a few songs. Nice! When Hurricane Gustav was headed toward Louisiana, the powers that be were evacuating the Beaumont area, where most of my family lives. I told everyone to come down to my place. Everyone stayed until it was safe to go home. That turned out to be the last time everyone got together there.

About two weeks later, Hurricane IKE was headed our way. On Thursday, IKE turned and headed directly at the Galveston/Bolivar Peninsula area. I came home from work early and had pretty much decided to miss the rush by leaving the next day since it wasn't going to hit until Saturday morning. I went down to the beach a couple times and the water had already covered up the beach and was coming into the neighborhood in between the dunes.

I packed three suits of clothes and a couple of other things. I left behind everything else. If I had stayed until Friday, like some did, I would not have been able to drive out. The Peninsula was already flooded a day before the storm made landfall.

I went to Leesville, Louisiana and got a hotel room. Saturday, after the storm, I decided to try to go home. It was not allowed of course. For two weeks, I waited, like everyone else did, to find out if I had anything. When I was finally allowed to go home, I found that I had a concrete slab, some piers and two palm trees left. Everything else was gone. I lost my favorite guitar that I had had for 20 years. My pictures. Everything. There were only a few houses in my subdivision, Gulf Shores that did survive, so I was not alone.

One year later, I have bought another house. My property at the beach has a "For Sale" sign on it. I am going to buy another beach cabin, I'm not sure when or where, but it will happen. I may even move back to Bolivar and start that business that I wanted to before the storm. I will find my way back to the coast where I belong.

Crystal Beach, Texas may not have been my hometown, but it will always be my home!!

JEAN BLOCK

"Thank you God for our lives!"

When we watched the news and heard that Hurricane IKE was coming this way, we decided to stay at Carol's "Bed and Breakfast" in Crystal Beach. We thought we would be safe there if IKE didn't get too bad.

Carol, Diane (my best friend), Misty and Cody (Carol and Diane's dogs) and myself went to Carol's on September 10, 2008. We planned to stay there until IKE was gone.

We watched the news and the news was telling everybody to leave the beach because IKE was going to be a big and bad "Hurricane."

We waited a while when we got to Carol's before we decided to go to High Island or Winnie. We finally decided to drive to Winnie, but the water was across Highway 87 and the Ferry was closed so we had no choice but to go back to Carol's.

Carol called the Coast Guard and asked, "If we left could we take our dogs on the Helicopter?" And a very rude woman said, "No, dogs weren't allowed on the helicopter!" So Carol told her, "In that case we will stay where we are, we aren't leaving our dogs."

A helicopter came to Carol's later and the pilot said, "We should leave before it's too late and he was sorry that we couldn't take the dogs on the helicopter." We told him, "We aren't leaving without Cody and Misty so we are staying no matter what!" He said, "Good luck" and we thanked him for his concerns.

Carol had a generator to use when the power went off. The news told everybody to fill up their bathtubs with water to use when they cut the water off, so we did. We hunkered down and prepared to stay and do the best we could to prepare for IKE

A member of the Task Force brought us a case of drinking water and some rations and he said, "We really should think about leaving", and Carol told him, "We would if we could take our dogs on the helicopter and we are not leaving Misty and Cody!"

We thanked him for the water and k-rations and we hoped for the best and we did a lot of praying.

IKE came in on Saturday morning, September 13, 2008 at 2:30 A.M. with winds at 115 miles an hour and a surge of 20 feet.

We were nervous, but we tried to stay calm and we prayed together often. Water came in on the second floor through a window where we were sleeping because the frame around the window came loose. The water went over the top of Carol's deck; she lost part of her deck, a fence downstairs, everything in her garage, a golf cart and her car. The car was stuck in the mud upside down next to her beach house.

Tracy Byrd, the famous country singer, lived in back of Carol. He lost part of his siding off his house, a jeep and his golf cart.

We watched a house in back of Carol's, close to the beach slowly go down to the ground with the wind and surge. Before the storm, Carol never had a view of the beach, but now she did. The houses all around hers were critically destroyed or completely gone!

We had seen a lot of debris and golf carts floating by during the Hurricane. Gilchrist, Crystal Beach and Canal City were pretty well wiped out. There were 3 or 4 houses on Highway 87 that withstood the hurricane. They were called the "bird houses" because they were built so high. There was maybe one house left in Canal City. All of the businesses on Highway 87 were destroyed.

Diane and I lost everything we owned in Canal City including my car. A member of the Task Force came to Carol's on Sunday, September 14th and told us, "We had to leave, they were searching for bodies." He had his truck parked on Highway 87 where the water had gone down. He told us, "We could walk to the road where the truck was parked and he would take us to Fort Travis Park where the helicopter is to take us to a shelter in Galveston." We were only allowed to take one suitcase and we COULD take Cody and Misty. They were NOW allowed on the helicopter which made us very happy. I was limping when I got out of the truck, (I need a knee replacement), and the two pilots from the helicopter made a chain and carried me to the helicopter. I felt like a queen!

The helicopter flew us to the shelter in Galveston. The man in charge of the shelter said, "The shelter was full, we would have to go to the shelter in San Antonio at Lackland Air Force Base." A bus took us to San Antonio. There was a special bus for people that had dogs. When we arrived in San Antonio the man in charge said, "There was already over ten thousand people in the shelter, but we still have room for more people." He also said, "They would have to put Cody and Misty in a kennel." Carol and Diane said, "There is no way, we are going to put them in a kennel!" (I didn't blame them!)

I told the man in charge, "I have somebody coming to get us." He said, "Are you sure? You really should stay here." I said, "Yes, I am sure, my son lives in Spring Branch, he will be glad to come get us." The man said, "Okay, just go sit over there and don't go anywhere."

We got to my son's place on September 15, 2008 in the morning just in time for my son to go to work. I stayed with my son, daughter-in-law and grandkids. Diane's son from Tyler came and picked her up. Carol stayed in a motel until her daughter from Mexico came to get her.

I registered with FEMA on September 22, 2008. I heard from them within a few weeks and I received a direct deposit into my account.

My health was getting worse after the Hurricane, so my son asked me to stay in Spring Branch near him and his family. I had nothing to go back to on the beach, so I decided to settle close by. I rented a nice trailer not too far from them. I miss Diane, (my best friend), I love her very much and I consider her a part of my family.

Diane is in a FEMA trailer in Lumberton and Carol is back at her "Bed and Breakfast" in Crystal Beach.

My two sons were worried about us until they knew we were safe. They stayed on the computer night and day until they talked to us. The news media was very evasive about informing people of the damage done to the Bolivar Peninsula. The news seemed more interested and worried about the damage done to Galveston. I don't think Galveston got any where the damage that "Bolivar" received and the lives that were lost.

We had people telling us we were crazy for staying on the beach during the Hurricane and I guess we were, but I thank God everyday for taking care of us and hearing our prayers.

A lot of our friends lost their lives and my heart goes out to the family and friends of those people. I visited Diane before Christmas and she took me to the beach. It looked like a "war zone." She also took me to Canal City where my house use to be. All that was left was the pilings. I took pictures, I was devastated. Thank God…Carol, Diane, Cody, Misty and I are safe and I am able to write about the experience we went through with IKE. I came out of it safe and able to pick up the pieces and go on with my life. I look forward to a bright future and better things to come to us with prayers and God's help.

We did a lot of praying and God answered our prayers! I am just so sorry that so many of our friends lost their lives. I pray that nobody in the world ever has to go through a Hurricane that Bolivar Peninsula and the people that lived there went through. "Thank you God for our lives!" Jean Block.

TRISH WHITE

"That's my story and I am sticking to this!"

I've been coming to the Bolivar Peninsula since I was a kid, Dirty Pelican and Meacom's Piers were a weekend trip. I blame by Dad for turning me into the "beach-bum," that I am today. I have only been fortunate to call this place home for the last five years. From day one everyone I have met has opened their hearts and they have always been there. Since the storm, there are many of you that I now get to call "true friends." Before this Hurricane we call IKE, I thought my dreams had come true… living the beach life! I was the new owner of a restaurant – bait-shop. I was two weeks from opening, as some of you know… the old Genie Bell's…."Lafitte's Hide Away" was the new name; it would have been.

I stayed through the last three storms we had and I almost stayed for IKE. I owe my life to JaDean, calling me all day on Thursday crying and begging and making me promise that I would leave. I left that evening, got a room in Winnie, Thanks, Studio 6, for everything.

They gave everyone until noon on Friday to evacuate, so I woke up and decided to drive back to get a few more things out of my place. I drove to High Island sometime around 7:00 A.M. or so, the water was already to Highway 124, coming up to the "Famous Fruit Stand." People I knew, too many to list, you all know who and remember too well being air lifted, wading through the water and hanging on to one another. I was hearing the stories of people trying to drive out through the treacherous water. The looks on everyone's faces… I'll never forget! Shortly afterwards, the officials were making everyone leave High Island.

Going back to Winnie, I ran into people who told me that this person or that person stayed realizing they would have to ride out the storm. There are some people we lost, including "Pee-Wee" and there are people still missing today, like Sandy. I was able to get back on the Peninsula the Tuesday after the storm, I drove through High Island and debris was everywhere. The last house on the right was gone, (I always loved that one), on the way down Highway

87, all I could say was, "Oh, my God!" There were cars tossed and crushed out in the pastures, the road was buried under sand and wash-out in many places. Thank God, I had a truck, I don't know if I could have made it through. I passed the piers and there was not one house. Well, the "Bird Houses" were still standing but they were hit hard. I drove towards Gilchrist, my heart stopped, the devastation before my eyes…I have never seen such! ….no church, no post office, no fire station… everyone's homes were gone! The whole town was gone! The bridge was gone on one side, so they wouldn't let anyone across. I walked to the end of the cut, where my restaurant/bait shop was…it was gone, Lafitte's gone. I just stood there; I couldn't breathe, think or cry. I just stood there looking at everyone's things that were scattered. It looked like our town was hit by a bomb, not a Hurricane. It was so unbelievable!

It was or seemed forever before I could get back on the Peninsula. They were rebuilding the bridge at Rollover Pass. When I did get to come back on, the place still pretty much looked the same. As I drove to Crystal Beach along the way so many houses were gone. You couldn't even place where things once stood. The Chevron was just a shell as if someone blew the front right off. Businesses gone, but the signs still there (you two know, miss you!) Houses had been washed into the Highway, along with boats and golf carts; it was all so crazy. I made my way to Bolivar, it was the same, (sorry Milt's, miss you too!) All day I just drove the Peninsula trying to find my favorite spots and my friend's homes. Some were there, some were gone….it was so hard to believe, (and still is!)

I have been through a few storms and remember some that hit the Peninsula, but nothing – nothing like this after losing everything. I still wanted to come back, a lot of my friends and family couldn't understand. I just know this place had become my home. It will never be the same as a lot of us remember, but with all of our memories we will make new ones to add to the old. A lot of us have had to fight and some still are, I could write a book on people's struggles. It is really sad, because of the Bolivar Peninsula's devastation, somehow we have been forgotten. I wonder where our Opera's, Brad Pitt's and morning updates are; the one thing that still sits in my heart one year later. From all the "mucky mud", the living here and living there…boy, do I and my new found "true friend," Katie have stories of our adventures on the Peninsula after the storm. The times of trying to leave before curfew, driving through what looked like ghost towns! There was the beach, ocean and waves on the road with us at times "scary."

I remember the first night the Peninsula got lights back…we were breakin' curfew, "Thanks William!" It was so odd, driving down Highway 87, I called Katie and asked, "Doesn't something look different?"….We had gotten so used to darkness it was almost strange to have lights again. After months, I made it home, "Thanks, Dab." "Boo-Hoo" for those still not back…and "Hats off" to High Island and Winnie-e-e for being back!! What a year it has been, that's for sure!

There has been a lot of talk about closing…. excuse me, filling in the Rollover Pass. When I heard that I wrote this: "Hurricane IKE came ashore one day to only take dreams and lives away. It has left me asking, why? There was once a town, Gilchrist, on that 32 mile stretch of land. Now all that left is sand, a drift and everyone's things scattered among. What's missed, some now want to forget that town, but I want to see it stick around. Even some locals don't care, but what they don't understand, if it wasn't for that Famous Fishing Spot…. We wouldn't have had the people travel here so many miles, some more than you know, only to help this Peninsula grow. This place we all call home, so as a whole, let's come together and don't forget that fishing spot and Gilchrist that some of us miss.

Through the pass of everything I want to say, "Thank you again to all who have been there: Henry – Katie – Fred… "Right on"… "True That." I will always love each and every one of you! To all that we have lost and to all that made it through the storm. It will suck to not have you all to make new memories with. Phish hold on, (be a part of the new one's), Laurel and the Electric Circus just came to town – "Keep those dancing shoes on"….as for this year IIWII!

WESLEY MOORE

"I STAYED, I SWAM…I SURVIVED"

I was in my house on Crystal Beach Road and the water started flowing into the house. The storm surge was coming in and it was taking out the front row houses…it was like a domino effect.

Shortly, after midnight a huge wave slammed another house into mine. My floor started to buckle and the door busted in along with a huge blast of water, mud, lumber and stuff. I knew I had to get out or I was going to drown. I couldn't get out of there fast enough, I swam out and then something caught my pants. I was trying to swim up and I was being pulled back. I saw a huge wave coming, it must have been 30 feet tall…it was huge! I lost my pants and swam up. I tried to swim with the flow; I knew not to swim against the current. I saw steel beams, tin sheets, metal rods, wood beams, lumber, etc. everywhere. I knew that if I got trapped in this I would be like a "smashed bug!" I knew I needed to get away from all of the debris before it busted me open. I saw the tip of the pine tree in my yard. I was swimming on top of the water and I was up near the top of this tree!! I thought about the Court House, I remembered there was a cage around the generator. I thought if I could get there and stand on top of the cage I would be safe. I swam there and that was not a possibility! I looked up and God was not ready to take me. It was pitch black – total darkness…I thought I heard a helicopter…but then I realized it was the generator, gurgling as it was drowning in the water. The water was tossing me around like a toy boat! I saw lights somewhere around the Subway parking lot, I thought it was a helicopter again, but then I realized it was the lights from the cars, short-circuiting. They were also submerged underneath all of the water. I ended up around the American Grill and I saw a tree branch behind the restaurant. I forced my way toward it and almost missed it, but finally I was able to clench onto the branch. I was in the water swimming for 8+ hours. This is where I managed to stay for the remainder of the storm. I had snakes crawling around my arms; they were also trying to survive! The debris was flying everywhere. I kept thinking about my cats and I am hoping they found a high place and survived.

Finally, the next morning just after daybreak, The Coast Guard came to rescue me. For thirty years, I have always stayed and I have **never** been through anything like this!!!

TESSA TEDDER

"IKE was full of surprises!"

I could tell you about evacuating, or how much and what I lost or any and all the bad things that I/my family went through due to Hurricane IKE. Lord knows we have all seen our share of hard times over the last year. Instead I want to tell you about something that happened in the middle of what I call "hell" that I look back now on and just laugh.

I am a Volunteer EMT – B with Crystal Beach VFD/EMS. So I got to come in Tuesday after the storm and assist in the search and rescues. I can honestly say that it was truly an honor to meet and work with so many wonderful people that were helping with the recovery. I was assigned to search "Goat Island" by airboat with the operator of the boat, his name was Brandon. He is a former Marine from Oklahoma with the same sense of humor I have, so we got along great. Thank Heavens!

Thursday after the storm we were on Goat Island to search a house that was there. I recognized the house, as it had been right down the road from my parent's house. I hadn't heard anything about the owners, so we really didn't know what or who we may find. Because the house was sitting on a slant, Brandon went in first to make sure it was safe for me to enter. We entered the house in the living room and everything looked like it had been vacuumed sealed in its place. First, we check the kitchen and then Brandon headed down the hall. From my view the hallway was clear, so I was surprised to hear Brandon scream. He let out a gut wrenching scream like I have never heard before, and his face was ghostly white. Then I heard, "We have a child in here!"

My heart sank and I ran to where he was. All we could see was a small hand sticking out. It was wedged between the wall and the door. So we start trying to get things away from it only to see red. All I could feel was something cold and hard, no pulse. When we were finally able to get it free, we were shocked at what we had discovered.

We both looked at each other and laughed, for what we had thought was a child, was in fact a 3 feet tall plastic Santa Claus. That's right!!…we had found

Santa on Goat Island. Now, when I want to get mad or upset about Hurricane IKE…I just think of that and I laugh!!

TAMELLA BAKER

"God's Strength in Disasters!"

Three days following Hurricane Ike's landfall on the Texas Coast and four days after our daughter's family is air lifted off the Peninsula I talk to my nine-year-old granddaughter. I wanted to hear her version of the events so I feign ignorance.

"Oh, hi Nana, let me take the phone into the yard so I can talk to you."

So I walked with her to the yard delighting in the journey itself and knowing that we were going to have a private talk together. She informed me that she could talk as long as she wanted because her mom had charged the battery on the cell phone.

She started out telling me how very much she missed me and of course I explained how much I needed her too. "But," I asked. "Are you happy where you are?"

"Oh yes, Nana, I'm very happy here. Grandpa has a nice yard and there are two dogs next door." She told me their names and a brief history she'd learned from their uncle. She explained how the storm had knocked down the fences but her Grandpa and Daddy could build them when they got their two dogs, Ty and Roxy back. She described how her Aunt Elizabeth's kitten had grown into a big cat.

So after some details of her current situation I said, "Cheyenne, I haven't heard how you got to your Grandpa's house."

"You don't know how I got to Grandpa's house?" She asked, incredulous.

"No."

"Oh Nana, let me tell you all about that!! Did you know the water was deep and Daddy took a sheet and spray-painted it … 'Family of 4 need HELP!'… But no one came? And then Mama told us that the Coast Guard is coming for us and we need to be ready. Daddy prayed for our house and our pets and our neighbors and then Nana the water was coming over the highway and Daddy prayed that God would…you know like he did for Moses in the Bible? Daddy asked God to part the water and let our family reach the chopper safely. And

Nana, the water was over the road but when we stopped praying the water wasn't over the road anymore."

I'm now crying tears of thankful joy and I said, "Oh God loves us, oh so much."

"Yes he does!" She says and continues. "The chopper came to get us."

"Cheyenne, it came to get you on your porch?"

"Oh, Nana," She says with a huff. "I've got to go sit down and tell you the whole story. You don't know how they got us?"

I told her no because in truth I hadn't heard her version of the story. Already I'd learned details her momma had left out. And I wanted her version of this miraculous story. I want her to memorize this story in her mind. I want her to be able to make a monument in her heart that she can return to when the storms of life assault her.

So the story continues as she takes her seat in the yard. "Well, we saw the helicopter in the field and we had to walk through the field to the helicopter."

"The helicopter landed in your field?"

"No Nana," By now her voice has an urgency to tell it in detail. "The water was too deep to land." She pauses.

"What color was the chopper? How did you get in it?"

"Let me tell you. It was red and it dropped a … cage and Mommy and Sky got in first and they pulled them into the helicopter."

"Were you so afraid?"

There was a long reflective pause and then an awareness of the very odd occurrence where Cheyenne is concerned as fear often paralyzes this little girl.

"Nana, I wasn't afraid at all." Words can't describe the awe struck voice of this precious 9 year-old girl.

After a moment she continued, "Daddy held my hands and he never let them go…even when they pulled me in the helicopter Daddy held my hands."

"Did the chopper take you to Grandpa's house?"

"No, Nana it was big. Don't you know that? We went to Texas City and there were lots of people there. And one asked Daddy if the water was over houses yet and Daddy told him how it was getting bad. They showed us where to go and there were lots of people there."

"Were any of your friends there?"

"No there were kids but I didn't know them."

"So Grandpa came and got you there?"

"Yes."

"Cheyenne can you draw me a picture of that chopper? I know you're an artist and I'd like to have a picture of that."

"Okay I'll do that today."

I'm thinking it's time to hang up but she tells me about their shopping trip. She described in minute detail her pants and then she says, "And when you see me I've got this shirt for you. It's brown and it says BFF, (Best Friends Forever), and when you see me wear it you'll know I got it for you because Nana, you're my best friend forever! And I miss you."

"Oh Cheyenne, you're my best friend too! And I miss you like crazy. And when I see you again you're going to have to sit in my lap because I'm going to hug you for so long we won't be able to stand that long. I love you oh so much!"

"I love you too Nana, I can talk as long as I want to." I understood that she didn't want to let me go and in reality I didn't want to let her go either.

But soon after I heard our daughter's voice explaining that she needs to pay some bills by phone. I thanked her for letting Cheyenne call me. She explained that Cheyenne had wanted to call right after their shopping trip but her phone battery was dead. But then this busy young woman took the time to tell me her side of the shopping story, proving that events like these build monuments of faith.

Carinn said that when she reached the checkout line and saw the girls who had shopped with Elizabeth, there were two new Barbie's in the buggy. They needed clothes and toothbrushes but before she could say anything Elizabeth said she'd bought them for the girls.

Right there in a long checkout line Carinn was overcome with the memories from her own childhood when we lost everything to fire. The generosity and love of another teenager who provided a "pound puppy" that enabled her to return to school after losing everything.

I want to think that we have quite enough monuments but oh Lord; I never want you to stop building them in our hearts. "So why should I question when you call us to walk in a wilderness of trial."

Habakkuk 3: 17-19. ***Though the fig tree should not blossom and there be no fruit on the vines, though the yield of the olive should fail and the fields produce no food. Though the flock should be cut off from the fold and there be no cattle in the stalls, yet I will exult in the Lord, I will rejoice in the God of my salvation. The Lord God is my strength and He has made my feet like hinds' feet, and makes me walk on my high places.***

Trials by fire and now by water, but you are the same God always faithful and you will be glorified as we walk through this trial in your strength! May you receive glory and honor as we tell and retell of your goodness and mercy forever!

PAMELA GOZA

"There was hope that all was not lost by IKE!"

I am fairly new to the immediate coast area, but not to Hurricanes. I grew up in Southeast Texas and moved to the coastline in November after Hurricane Rita. I lived in Port Bolivar until getting married on April 10, 2008 and moved to Galveston. I run two small companies that service the Bolivar Peninsula. Maid in Crystal Beach is a cleaning business that services private homes, beach rentals, construction and commercial properties. Care Partners is a private home care service for elderly and handicapped individuals. Needless to say, Hurricane IKE changed my life in extraordinary measures.

Around August 30, 2008, I had received word that a cabin had become vacant in Port Bolivar. At that time, I had my offices operating out of my house in Galveston, while storing my supplies and equipment in two storage units on the peninsula in Crystal Beach. Merging the two into one location made perfect sense. I began the transition one week prior to Hurricane IKE'S arrival. Both storage units were closed and I made daily trips with office furnishings during the course of the week. I spent the latter part of the week contacting our clients to see what their plans were for the impending hurricane. It seemed everyone was leaving except for my two employees, my husband and I. One employee lived in Crystal Beach where she and her husband planned to ride it out, while another employee went to her parent's house in High Island, the opposite end of the peninsula. My husband and I stayed on the island in our home, on Biovu Drive, also known as Farmer's Point, while all of our neighbors chose to evacuate.

On September 11, 2008, we were awakened by banging on our door. It was friends who came out to find water in the street. My husband moved his truck from the curb in the front of the house to the garage area in back of the house. We then checked the Internet for the latest coordinates of the storm and we decided to start taking precaution in the event the water came inside the house. We moved from room-to-room raising everything about six to eight inches off the floor. This action became a cyclical behavior for as soon as we finished elevating what we could, we checked the water level in the front yard, then started raising everything higher. Again and again, we did this until we had no other choice but to move the necessity things to the second floor. Out of concern for the fast rising water, we moved our vehicles inland to a bank that had just been built on an elevated mound. We pulled as close as we could to the building in hopes of keeping as much of the undercarriage dry as we could.

We locked up, looked around at everyone else doing the same as we had and began the long wade home through the water. Parts of our journey home, we waded in hip-high levels of water. By 4:00 P.M., the water was already up to my ribs; I am 5'3". Panic began to set in. Not about the storm itself, but this fast rising water and damage it is going to cause. We moved the last of our important documents, etc., upstairs. Still not convinced that the water will reach the second floor, we put our photo albums in the tops of two closets, my husband's in one room on the backside of the house, mine in our room on the front side of the house. Last to take upstairs was a few changes of clothing and shoes, our dog, Lily with her kennel and son's ferret in his cage.

Feeling restless, just waiting for the storm to make landfall when it was deceivingly beautiful outside, other than the water everywhere, we decided to take the boat out for a look around the neighborhood and check on anyone else who stayed behind. Amazing! Cars were already submerged, trucks continued to drive through the high water, with bubbles seen blowing from the exhaust as if they were being pushed by a propeller. Mail boxes were topped off by the water, but for the most part, everyone we passed was in great spirits. Smiling and laughing, not expressing any fears at all about Hurricane IKE.

By nightfall, we had about three feet of water inside our home. We watched from the balcony of the second floor as neighbor's property from their garages, back yards, and first floors began swiftly moving out of and away from their homes, consumed by Galveston Bay. Nothing could be done now to save anything. The water was too high and moving too fast. We stood helplessly watching years of assumption disappear in a matter of minutes. We moved to the roof of the first floor to get a better aerial view of the street and neighboring homes surrounding the backside of our house. A move that should have been a wakeup call, as the Coast or National Guard came hovering above us, urging us to allow them to air lift us up. Calmly, we waved them away, indicating we were okay. Never imaging this would prove to be a foolish move.

As darkness fell, we moved inside to wait for the storm. The winds picked up, but we could not really hear its wrath as the trees were not able to shake like they would have had they not had so much water surrounding them. We began hearing a noise, only to realize it was our garage contents hitting the ceiling of the first floor. The water was coming! We had a radio that ran off a battery and heard reports of fires around town, which we could verify ourselves by looking out the window. Red illuminated the sky and smoke could be smelled. Our thought shifted back and forth between, "well, if the storm doesn't get us, the fires will!" Crazy thoughts! Each time we came to the window to see the flames and smoke, we were reminded of the storm when waves passed about three feet from the window sill.

A repeating report about a female caller from Crystal Beach to "911" had my undivided attention each time the reporter made mention of the conversation. The caller reported that she knew no one could come out to get them in the middle of the storm, but she wanted them to know where they were and what was going on. She stated that her home had been swept away and she and her husband and some other residence had managed to make their way to Seaside Lumber and get to the roof. The water was that high and they were exposed to the elements of the storm. The group was going to try to get to the First Baptist Church and see if they could find a way inside as it was on elevated ground and was two or three stories high and she would call back if they made it. How terrifying!! I knew this had to be my employee, Christal. She lives down the street next to this lumber yard, closer to the beach. Next report that came in was they had miraculously made it to the church and was able to get inside the upper floors. The caller reported they also had a man staying there with his lion, but had to leave his tiger behind as it had already died in the storm's affects. I knew in my heart this was her. I had left cell phones with each employee and stated to keep in touch with me and let me know how you are and where you end up. It had to be her!!

Time did move quickly, however. The eye was over us before we realized it and seeing the first floor completely submerged and only three steps left before reaching the second floor told me we had a disaster declaration coming and I wasted no time in getting in touch with FEMA and get registered before all power and cell phone service was lost entirely. We were given the Red Cross number and told that as soon as the President made the Disaster Declaration, our information would be dropped into "the bucket." The operator didn't notice my giggle at her remarks. "Dropped into the bucket" was a little humorous with all this water around us.

The water level dropped considerable before the backside of the storm came through. This side was felt much more than the first half. IKE was alive and he was making his presence known in a very big way. The house never shifted off its blocks/piers, but the roar of the storm was literally inside the house with us and felt as if we were going to be buried alive. The front door had been torn from its hinges and the water and contents on the first floor would be completely sucked out of the house, then seconds later, the water, house contents, and other debris forced back inside, filling up the first floor as quickly as it emptied it. All of the sights and sounds of it all were horrifying. Once again, the water level began rising. This time, we were using towels to try and soak up as much of the water coming over the staircase into the second level of the house, to no avail.

There came a point when my husband and I, still calm, so it appeared on the outside, began thinking that maybe this WAS NOT such a good idea and because of our decision to stay, we were going to die. In a last ditch effort, we put garbage bags over us like raincoats and put life-jackets on over that. My husband wrapped duct tape around my jacket to make it tighter so it would not slip off in the swift waters of IKE. He tied our jackets together with a small rope then we sat on the sofa, waiting to see how much of our house IKE was going to consume. Lilly (dog) and Buddy (ferret) were very anxious throughout the whole ordeal, but we weren't leaving without them either. We had a double sided bag that allowed for Lilly to be put in one side and Buddy the other if we had to venture out into the water willingly or forced out. As we sat waiting, my husband sat back on the sofa and shut his eyes. Praying? I don't know. I just took the opportunity to scribble my social security on my arm so I could be identified in the event we didn't make it through the storm. I had my driver's license in my pocket, but didn't feel that would survive the wrath we were experiencing with IKE. When my husband sat up and saw what I had done, he was crushed that I would think he would let anything happen to me. I felt bad for his feelings, but quietly knew that if IKE wanted us, there was nothing my husband could do. He was way out matched.

Over and over I kept telling God, "Okay Lord! I had always hoped you'd take me in my sleep, cuz you know how I don't like pain. Buuutttt, if this is your plan on how I'm to get to you, I'll face it. OOOOOOHHHH, but it's going to hurt. Just let it be quick Lord!" I could visualize being ripped from the house, slammed against walls, stairs, doors, and sucked under the water hitting all sorts of other debris along the way. I did not look forward to it. The bright side of it would be, in a few minutes (hopefully minutes) I would be with the Lord.

Amazingly, the house held, we weren't swallowed by IKE, and the water was receding as quickly as it rose. When we were able to wade out, we walked downstairs to check the contents. IKE had pulled the walls off the front side of the house and the wall between the garage and the house itself was punctured. This explained how everything was washed away or relocated to another part of the house. Uncontrollable sobbing was all I could do. Years of possessions gone! Heavy contents that we thought would not move from its place were toppled over like it weighed nothing at all. One room's closet shelf not touched, my husband's photo albums rested there unscaved, while another closet's shelf contents ruined, this is where my photo albums rested no more. All is lost except for what we had on and what little moved upstairs. Numb and disbelieving we survived this catastrophe; we headed to the street for that watery hike to the bank where we had left our vehicles. We saw houses crumbled to the ground. Other houses not even there anymore. It looked more like a third-world country experiencing war or natural disaster…not America…not Texas…not Galveston County.

Sigh of relief when we saw our vehicles as we got closer and closer to the bank. They did not appear to have been moved by the water, but could not tell if water had gotten inside or not. Debris lay around and underneath them, so we left them there and began walking to check on my husband's family who was gathered there during the storm. Everyone seemed okay, just shaken by the experience. We wasted no time in getting back to the house to gather some things that we would need over the course of weeks to come. We had two generators there and both the animals. We had cans of gasoline on the balcony and some food in coolers. My brother-in-law drove us back to the bank to get my husband's truck. We drove it as close to the house as we could then opted to take a boat that we found on the road back the rest of the way to carry out our things. We took all that we could salvage at that time and headed back.

The following day was Sunday. Just as we always did on Sundays, my husband and I headed to church, although this time, we were wet, dirty and smelly. Not once were we embarrassed about our dress, just thankful to be alive. This was our first time to actually see the exterior of the island. It was indescribable. No words exchanged between us until we got to church and the doors were locked up tight. It was a ghost town!! Everywhere we looked, buildings were missing, destroyed or gutted by Hurricane IKE's Fury. The grass and trees were now brown, like they get in the dead of winter. No church today, anywhere!!

In the days to come, we contacted all of the insurance companies and stood in the long lines for information, food, water and ice. A routine I don't ever want to get used to doing ever again. By the next Sunday, there was still no word from FEMA or insurance companies. We again went to church, but again, no one there. Still locked up tight! I was desperate to attend and my husband searched the roads to find any church, any denomination, it didn't matter, that was having service and we found none. Feeling lost and believing everyone had forgotten GOD in all this mess, we headed to the distribution site to get our daily newspaper (page or two long) and handouts. What a blessing this little newspaper had become in lives. No other contact with the outside world at all except this thin little paper handed to us each morning. In it, we saw that Sacred Heart was having mass at the Hotel Galvez, in the ball room at noon. We attend nine o'clock mass normally so we were slightly early. We felt sure everyone remaining on the island would be making their way to service, but this was not the case. We waited more than two hours for mass and only a handful of people showed up. It seemed there were more reporters than service goers. I was glad to be among the few.

As days turned into weeks, credible word of the conditions of the Bolivar Peninsula was mixed. The local media reported dead cattle and people littered the area and all structures destroyed. The not actually knowing, seeing for myself, was adding to the anxiety and depression I was experiencing. My husband's employer, Farmer Marine, set up an RV park in the parking lot of their sister company Farmer Alloy and an employee lent us their travel trailer while getting back onto our feet. I had never stayed in a travel trailer before and I was most grateful for the outpour of generosity, but I began feeling trapped in such tight quarters. I was still crying daily and not sleeping, but maybe an hour or two at the most each night, reliving the night that IKE came ashore. Things only worsened when officials lifted the ban on entry to the peninsula and allowed us to return to our homes and businesses. My husband and I made the long trip from La Marque to High Island then up Highway 87 to Port Bolivar. From the time we came over the High Island hill and descended toward the coastline, tears rolled uncontrollably down my face. These were my people! Homes were gone from Highway 124 where they sat just days before. No debris; just gone! The roads were torn up with big chunks of asphalt missing. Sand covered the roads and both sides of the street where the road was exposed. For miles we drove in silence and saw nothing but sand, pilings and large divots where either asphalt or concrete once lay. It was unbelievably devastating to see "my people", "my roads", "my homes" and "my businesses" gone and replaced with sand. I couldn't tell where we were on Highway 87 until we reached the heavily damaged Rollover Pass Bridge. Uncontrollable sobbing was the only sound in the truck. I could barely catch my breath, it hurt so much! The devastation of Galveston was quite different from the devastation on Bolivar Peninsula. Galveston had debris everywhere….Here, in Gilchrist, there was nothing…Wiped off the face of the earth!

Seeing Crystal Beach was somewhat more hopeful of the survival of our community. The devastation was definitely present, but there were signs of life. Some houses and building were still standing! The hurting I felt was no less painful however, but it gave me hope seeing that not all was lost by Hurricane IKE. As we traveled further up the peninsula toward the Ferry landings, I kept telling myself maybe we would see even less chaos. With each turn we saw damage to our neighbor homes, but they were still there. I had managed to pull myself together while riding through the neighborhood, but as we turned on 15th street, seeing the cabin that I had rented for the offices of Care Partners and Maid in Crystal Beach still standing produced a flood of tears for joy. It survived!! A couple of pieces of siding and shingles were missing. The garage doors were damaged, but still worked. When we walked inside, everything was still in the exact place we had left it; undamaged by the wrath of IKE. We had a place to call home after all. Hurricane IKE hadn't taken everything from us.

Leaving the peninsula before curfew was difficult. I returned as often as I could that week, but my mental health was still deteriorating. I could not shake the PTSD that the medical team at UTMB stated I was experiencing. I left the area around September 28, 2008 to "get away from it all." I hadn't noticed the amount of weight loss experienced until I arrived at my daughter Stephanie's house and instead of "Hello," I was welcomed with, "Oh, my God." That was the first time since the storm that I laid my head down and slept. I slept for eight to ten hours straight. I finally felt safe. After a couple of days getting to know my new grandbaby, Taylor Grace, we went sightseeing on the coast from Hamshire, La Belle, Fannett, Port Arthur, Groves, Bridge City and Sabine Pass. We spent another day just driving up and down the streets of the peninsula, recalling where clients and friends once lived and taking as many pictures of the area as we could. My stay in Silsbee was short. When I began recognizing that the "lotion" that I had been putting on my skin after being burned by whatever was in the water I waded through to get out of my house was actually "exfoliating bath wash!" I figured I had rested enough and it was time to get back in the saddle and start getting on with recovery and rebuilding my life!

NORMA JEAN HEDGER

"No storm can tear away my memories of Bolivar!"

I remember back in 1961, my husband, Ace had repaired and elevated our home after Hurricane Carla. His boat and our home have survived all of the storms since. His Alzheimer's safe return medical bracelet has taken him safely home for the final time. I will remain in Pennsylvania with my family for the foreseeable future.

There is a time and a season for everything.

To those of you who can and are repairing, rebuilding and fixing Bolivar: Change, growth and progress are necessary. Do not let it grow too fast or too BIG. Keep what you all love about that "small, local fishing village across the pond from Galveston." Things can be replaced, people and pets cannot. Make your new places homes, not houses, know your neighbors, watch out for each other, know who is who, where they belong or don't belong, get rid of the transient scammers, don't let the beauracrats take over. Treasure your new times and seasons in Bolivar.

Memories of Business/Banking/Money Exchange in Bolivar:

As recently as the early 1990's there was no ATM at the bank, none of the stores took credit cards, you paid cash, wrote a check or just signed your name and paid your bill next time you were in or when you got paid. Personal checks were accepted and cashed by Hughes' (the Bolivar Market), Floyd's (McDaniel's Convenience Store) and the Hornbeck's (Milt's Seafood Market) for no fee and with no I.D. Payroll checks from everywhere were cashed at Fisherman's Cove, (The Indian Store), for a 1% fee. Jay and Rose were "the Indian's," no limit, no bankers hours, an advance call was appreciated when a bunch of big boats were coming in, but, even without warning, everyone got their checks cashed or the Captain cashed a big check and it was divided to the crews. They all gripped about the 1% but would rather pay it than drive to Crystal Beach even during bank hours or wait until the next day. The safes were "walk-in's" and better than a lot of banks with backup from the house in the back.

If you really needed money you could always go to the fish houses, (Hornbeck's, Blume's and Pat Henry at French Town.) Many of the boat Captains and business owners had in-home safes. In a pinch you knew where to go for ready cash.

There was NO robbing those folks. As the book written years ago, is so aptly named, "They Made Their Own Law."

Groceries, materials and boat supplies were charged until the next trip or job. Peggy at the Net Shop and Harry Hughes and family would bail anyone out in a pinch.

If you wrote a bad check, Floyd called Jay, Jay called Harry, Harry called Jimmy and Johnny, then they all called the Big Store, which was not yet the big store, the other boat docks, DeFonti's Shipyard, Laura Lee and Evelyn Ann at the hair salons, and out went the word. You did not want your name to be on the list Floyd kept posted, in plain view, on his wall or in the little flip notebooks at Fisherman's Cove or Hughes'. One time, Floyd had a neon sign with the names of folks who wrote bad checks and owed him money on the front of his store.

I worked for Floyd in 1996/1997 and Fisherman's Cove 1997/1999. As hard-nosed as they acted, even Floyd and Jay & Rose would let people charge groceries and supplies and sometimes take and/or cash personal checks they knew would never be repaid. The unpaid charge bills and bad checks were in the tens of thousands that I have personal knowledge of in those two small stores alone. The businesses still made profits. The local's with no money, no credit, bad credit, no bank account, no I.D., etc. had food, clothing, heat and what was needed. The only thing that was totally taboo was STEALING.

People knew those hanging out in front of the stores and at the docks. You knew when they were telling the truth about being broke, losing money, not having work or just bumming and/or scamming for the next drink or dope. You made your decision to help or not help knowing who was who, where they lived or didn't (in a tent on the beach,) what vehicle they drove, bike they rode or if they walked, you knew who was who and what was what. The joke was "Bolivar has its quota of bums, we know who they are, they are basically harmless, we support them, and we are not taking in anymore."

Changes were happening before IKE. The population expansion, building of retirement and resort homes, more tourists, new, modern businesses, more of the unsavory "gypsies, tramps and thieves" that come with growth, longer ferry lines, codes, laws, and the BPSUD dictatorship. All those and more were taking their toll on the little fishing village. The "Big City Folks" with their "Town" ideas bringing the "Big City" and "Town" with them.

"Old Bolivar" was hanging on. Most of the small local stores and businesses were still doing business with locals the way they always had and making some of the changes demanded by the new population.

Then IKE......The most devastating part of what IKE did, was the many people who lost their lives in the storm. Many pets, livestock and other animals lost their lives. Since the storm, several long time residents and what I call, "The Old Bolivar Bulls," C.W. Kahla, Bernard Guidry and Ace Hedger have "gone home." Others have moved away, never to return. Some, who are still in Bolivar, are in declining health and cannot rebuild as they once could.

Along with most homes, those small businesses I mentioned were destroyed. Who is to rebuild them? If/when they are rebuilt; I doubt the Business and Banking/Money Exchange of Bolivar's past will return.

I am blessed by the memories of people, places and the way of life that was Bolivar in the time I spent there. I am even more blessed having known some of the "Old Bolivar Bulls" and hearing the stories that Captain Ace and his friends told of the Bolivar they grew up in. It is irreplaceable! No storm or loss can tear away the memories.

MICHAEL CLOW

"I saw, I swam, I struggled and I managed to survive!"

On Friday, September 12, 2008 around 9:00 A.M., I looked down the street and I could see the water. By noon, I was standing waist deep in the water. Around 6:00 P.M., I was forced to start swimming and by 9:00 P.M., I was trying not to drown.

My house was built out of cinder blocks, it was starting to break apart and crumble into pieces. I had to try to swim to my neighbor's house. I was struggling in the water far above my head. I had to save my two kittens, so I had put them in the cooler along with some cigarettes and a stash of beer. I floated on this cooler. I said to myself, "You are either going to die or you are going to get to that house!" I kept thinking, If only I had one of my kites. The kite could take me there. I have always loved the sport of flying kites!

I swam for over 4 hours in 15 feet water and I did make it to my neighbor's house. It was odd, the water was warm, probably 80 degrees. I rode out the remainder of the storm in the house. I saved my kittens, we all survived! The house I stayed in took on a lot of damaged. The storm took nearly half of it; however, I managed to stay safe within it!

No one knows what it was actually like to have stayed during this storm. Everyone talks about losing this or losing that. However, they didn't go through the fear that I went through. They didn't have the fear of drowning, the fear of trying to stay alive. They did not see what all I saw during that night! And yes, I lost everything, but I survived! So when I hear people talking about losing their material things, I just think to myself, "They were safe somewhere....they can't even begin to imagine what it was really like!"

After the storm, my neighbor, Pam told me I could stay at her house, (the one I rode the storm out in), until I got my feet on the ground. Everyone kept coming to the house wanting to interview me. I was interviewed by the N.Y. Times, the Houston Chronicle (twice) and the Galveston Daily News. FEMA was no help to me! I finally bought a camper and I am living in it at this time. I am still flying kites! I just want you to know…I never, ever want to ride out another Hurricane like that!

LINDA WILSON

"IKE took its toll on our lives forever!"

For me, it all began Wednesday evening with friends I was visiting. We sat in front of their television for what seemed like hours for us. We were watching the storm approaching closer and closer. About 2:00 A.M. that Thursday morning we all finally went to bed exhausted. My friends wanted me to spend the night so that I wouldn't be alone. About 5:00 A.M. I woke up to hear my friends discussing our evacuation plans. They could tell by the look on my face that I was terrified. Calmly they told me to go back to my home and gather up as much as I could and come back to their home.

My boyfriend at that time was out of town on a job so not only did I have to grab my personal belongings at my home, but also those at his home where we had lived together for six years. We had between us two vehicles to move plus his parrot and my dog. His son and two of his friends came by around noon to board up windows. We started our convoy to my boyfriend's parent's home in Vidor, Texas. There, his parents and brother and I waited. Around 1:00 A.M. Friday morning I woke up to very strong winds shaking the house. Then, the electricity went out. We all gathered in the living room not knowing then what had happened on the Peninsula. Later in the day, around 5:30 P.M. my boyfriend made it home to his parents with food and supplies. His brother was able to pull up on his laptop pictures of the devastation to the Peninsula. Nothing was left of Gilchrist where we lived. For the first time I saw my boyfriend cry. He and I had lost everything. We stayed with his parents until Monday and then moved his 5th wheel camper to a camp-site nearby. There we lived until the stress of the storm and past issues consumed us. We broke up the end of October. I left and moved in with my son in Beaumont for six months.

I began coming back to the Peninsula in February on the weekends and staying at Joy Sands Motel. Coconut's Restaurant was across the Highway and was a gathering place daily and nightly for me. I began to see more and more familiar faces. Oh, by the way I forgot to mention that my home made it in Port Bolivar. I knew in February I was coming back home, but not quite sure just when and how. I had sub-leased my home for a year. I made up my mind to move back to the Peninsula on April 1, 2009. I found a trailer to rent and there I stayed until September 1, 2009 when I was able to move back into my home. The one good thing that came out of IKE for me was being able to spend 6 months with my son and his wife and my two precious grandbabies. That was a blessing. I am so thankful that my home made it, but at the same time I felt guilty because so many of my friend's homes didn't make it. All I know is that we here, on the Bolivar Peninsula are so strong. Our stories right after the storm had even some of the FEMA inspectors crying. They told us that they had never seen such devastation before, but also said that the people here were the strongest, sweetest and the most caring people that they had ever come across. That meant so much to me because I know it is so true. We have come so far in such a short time. I never would have believed it if I hadn't seen it with my own eyes. Thanks to the many people who came to help bring Bolivar Back! A special thanks to Pamela Couch who kept us all updated on her website before we could come back home. Life for me is getting better, but for all of us, IKE took its toll on our lives forever!

VICKIE LEE CASH

"Home Sweet Home!"

IKE changed my life and my world. A dozen years ago, the beach house on Stingaree Road was the next best thing to living on a boat!

In May of 1998, we bought an old Shell Shop and started a business. It was right across the street from the Baptist Church in Gilchrist. Over the years I have met lots of interesting people. I have been out on many different boat rides. I have learned how to find 10,000 year old black sharks teeth and I have made a lot of jewelry with my findings. I have found all of them on the shoreline of the Bolivar Peninsula. Throughout the years, I have been known to sell various things especially Mary Kay Cosmetics and crafts involving sea shells.

That weekend before the storm, in September 2008 a group of friends and I had planned a trip to the Niagara Falls. Of course we all had to cancel our traveling plans, because IKE was predicted to bring heavy rain on almost all of the USA.

I evacuated to Oklahoma City and stayed at my mom's house. While I was there, I constantly watched the news stations and the internet for anything I could find on the Bolivar Peninsula. The media wasn't showing enough, I had to come back to Bolivar to see for myself. Upon entering the Peninsula, I found it so very hard to see anything through the tears, as I drove through Winnie, then High Island, then Gilchrist and the Rollover Pass. "Unbelievable," words cannot even describe the emotions, thoughts and memories, that were replaying over and over in my head. My lot on Dolphin road in Gilchrist was drying out and the road was okay to drive on. "Again, so Unbelievable!" the feeling of the knowledge of 10 – 14 feet of water was right here. It was sure good to see familiar faces at different events. Also getting together and running into friends in Winnie at the stores. It felt so nice and made me feel more content to see my friends and to talk about all of our adventures of a life time.

On January 8, 2009 we moved back to the beach in Caplen. We are in a 5th wheel 39 feet trailer on our slab. We had water and we used a generator for electricity. There was no one else around, no lights except for ours. It was very dark and pretty quiet. It was very difficult getting our mail. At first, I went to Stowell to get the mail then I had to pay for a box in Crystal Beach.

There was water, food and cleaning supplies in the Methodist church parking lot. It was greatly appreciated. I sure was glad when the Big Store opened up!

It has been 10 months since I have been back to the beach. It has been very challenging and emotional to deal with life with all of the changes. Life is a changing adventure and I thank God for being with me every step of the way.

I will always love the Beach! VickieLeeCash@yahoo.com

RANDY MATTES

"It's been an adventure!"

On Friday, September 12, 2008, I was planning on staying. I have ridden out many storms in the past years. My apartment sits above the Latitude 29 Surf Shop; it is about 12 feet high and very stable. Early that morning Rusty called me and told me that the storm is worst than we all thought and that I should pack up some of by belongings and meet them at the Mini Storage Units. He said we are going to try to find a way off the Peninsula. I met with several others at the storage units. It was too late to drive off the Peninsula, so I parked my truck on the hill at the 1st Baptist Church. The flood waters had never gotten that high before, so I figured it would be safe there for a few days until I could come back.

I had cleaned out my freezer and brought shrimp and steak to the storage unit…just in case we had to "ride out" the storm there. I really didn't know why I left my safe apartment, but it was great being with buddies. Later that morning, we were starting to get flooded out at the storage units and we all moved to the Crenshaw Elementary School. We also got "news" that we might have a helicopter coming to pick us up.

As the choppers were getting ready to land, I helped one of my friends with one of their dogs…to get the dog towards and on the helicopter. It was a challenge; the dog did not want to go! In the midst of all of this, I dropped my cell phone in the flood waters below the chopper trying to get us all on. My cell phone had all of my contacts and all of the numbers that I didn't know from memory. However, I could not get off the chopper to retrieve it or I'd get left behind.

We took the helicopter to Texas City and from there we took an evacuation bus to Austin. Ralph, a new buddy of mine, and I decided we would get and share a hotel room, (which was the only room left in Austin and it was $250.00 a night!), so we gladly took it!! We then planned things out; got some rest and the next morning we rented a car and drove to Ralph's family's house near Dallas. We stayed at their house for about a week. All of my friends were worried about me, because they could not reach me via my cell. They all thought I had stayed and they imagined the worst. I finally got in touch with some of my friends and they were planning to take a boat across to the Peninsula. I hooked up with them and we took the boat over; we walked a few miles to the First Baptist Church to retrieve my truck. It was so exciting, it cranked right up. We drove it down towards Tidelands subdivision, where a lot of our "Spec houses" were…we were in "awe" the whole time with all of the destruction. Words could not even begin to describe it! We made it to Tidelands, and one of the "Spec houses" was still standing, so we got the generator out of the back of my truck and to my amazement, it cranked right up!! We drove my truck back to the boat and left the Peninsula; it had been a long day!!

That evening with hooked up with Channel 11 and made plans to take one of the news reporters on the boat with us the next morning. We all made it across fine and got in my truck and drove around the Peninsula. I kept hearing terrible "skretching noises" coming from my truck. We were miles away from the boat and I was worried we might all have to walk back. I opened up the hood and noticed the air fan motor was not turning. I decided to turn off my truck to prevent a "belt" from breaking, while I looked for something to fix the motor. I found something, and gave the motor a good hit…it starting turning!! We drove back to the boat safely.

My apartment was fine…I was only missing the deck and stairs. The upstairs looked the same as when I had left it! Oh course, the surf shop below was completely destroyed. There was ½ of the roof gone, one end of the store was completely caved in and all of the merchandise that was still inside was trashed.

I ended up living in one of the "spec houses" for about 4 months, because we had several generators and it was closer to my work. I ended up letting, Craig, one of our hired hands, stay in my apartment. My truck only made it about a month and then it completely locked-up on me from all of the salt water and rust. I finally had stairs put on my apartment in March and began living back in MY HOME. It has been an adventure during this past year…but it is home!!

JUDY AND ELMER HAY

"Would they return?"

On February 25, 2009 while trying to restore our beach house this event took place!

It was one of the questions pondered.
Not at the top of our worries;
But definitely on the list.
After the hurricane, with all their homes destroyed,
Would the Purple Martins return?

It was time for the scouts.
We had heard some had been spotted.

Late afternoon, me on the deck
Elmer perched on a ladder from roof to deck.
A small search party of scouts swooped over the peak of the roof.
Like miniature helicopters, they hovered ten feet above Elmer's head.
They rotated their tiny heads and shouted:
"Hey, Dude, we're back. What the hell happened here?"
(*Sorry about the language; that's just the way those scouts talk.*)

Elmer shrugged…."I didn't do it."

Off they soared; only to return minutes later.
Before they could start up again with their cussin' and fussin',
Elmer shouted, "Get over it! We've built a new house for you…Everything
                will be alright."

A few moments of quiet
And they seemed to agree
As they darted away.

JUDY HAY

"Ten things to Remember while Re-storing your Beach House!" 6/09

10.) It will cost twice as much and will take 3 times as long.

9.) You can use the dead oleander bush as a toilet for a lot longer than you ever imagined.

8.) Don't agree with your insurance that you need any doors or windows.

7.) There will never be another day in your life when there isn't something to fix.

6.) Don't be in a hurry.

5.) No matter what, get the new Purple Martin house up in time.

4.) Bleach and water are your new perfume.

3.) A continuous burning debris pile is a good thing.

2.) Now that you are front row for awhile, remember to enjoy the view.

1.) And the #1 thing to remember when restoring a beach house is….

There will always be sand in the walls and sand under the floors!

As a kid I visited relatives with a beach house behind Swede's Grocery store. My father was the 1st to build in Crenneland in 1964 and my husband built on Salt Cedar Lane in 1993.

The following 6 stories are written by Ms. Parson's third grade class at the Crenshaw Elementary School in Crystal Beach, Texas.

JESSICA LOPEZ

"I am glad to be home."

On September 10, 2008, when I got home from school, my parents told me that Hurricane IKE was coming closer. My mom told us that she already had our stuff packed up. I went to get my pet and its food. I went to my sister's room and got my make-up and hats. My parents asked me if I had my dog and I said, "Yes." I asked my dad if I could take the pool and he said, "No", because he said nothing would happen to it. I said, "OK, Dad." I asked my mom where we were going, but she did not answer. I got diapers for my baby sister, Karla. I asked my mom if she packed all of our stuff including underwear and socks. My mom said she did. I felt sad because I didn't want to leave my home.

I didn't know who or what to play with in the car because I forgot to bring my toys. It was boring in the car. I didn't know what to do. Finally, along the way, we got to a store and my dad put gas in our car. I went inside the store and bought some bubble gum. We left the store and two hours passed, my dad was driving and my mom was taking care of my baby sister. My other sisters were asleep. My aunt called us to see if we were going to her house and my mom said we were. They told us that they had room in their house, so my mom asked my dad if he wanted to go and he said, "Yes." Finally we arrived in Longview. My mom called my aunt back so we could get directions on which road they lived on. They said that they were waiting for us. We found them because they called us again and said they had a dark green hummer. We followed them home and their house looked like they were rich, but they weren't.

We were there about two weeks when my Aunt took us to the mall. She bought Sonia some fancy boots and then she took us to Ross and bought Yuridia a dress and it was pretty. She bought me two pairs of brand new sandals. She bought all of us hair bands and a lot of other hair stuff.

The days passed and finally we heard the news and that hurricane IKE left everything destroyed on the Bolivar Peninsula. My mom was the one listening because I didn't want to hear about it. I missed my home. About two months passed and it was November 2008. My parents said they had to go to Houston and I spent the night with my aunt. I cried because my mom and dad were leaving. Come to find out, my parents were going to check on our house.

I went to school in Longview. It was called Bramlette Elementary School. The first day I was crying because I didn't want to leave my mom. I was scared. We had to wear uniforms to school. Their colors were red, white and blue, but I didn't have to wear a uniform to school at first because I didn't have one. My mom had to buy uniforms for us. Yuridia and I had to go to the same school. Sonia had to go to a different school called Parker Middle School. When we got home from school, we were crying. I didn't like the school in Longview even though my teacher was nice. My teacher's name was Mrs. Hamalten. She was a great teacher. We had a lot of kids in our classroom. Our principal was Mrs. Barnet. She was a woman.

We returned to the Peninsula on December 15, 2008. My mom registered us at High Island School in High Island. My teacher's name was Mrs. O'Leary. She was nice. I didn't know that much about High Island. The school looked big like Crenshaw, but it wasn't. I got to know the principal. He was a man named Mr. Taket. There wasn't a nurse there. When we got home I told my mom that I didn't like High Island. My mom told me to forget about it that it was the only school on our Peninsula or if we wanted to we could go to East Chambers. I said, "Definitely, not East Chambers, Mom." I did feel bad because I missed my home and I wished my house didn't get water inside. My parents went to check on our house and took pictures.

Finally, Crenshaw Elementary on the Peninsula opened on February 4, 2009. I asked my mom if she could fill out the papers for us to go to school there. She said, "YES." I was excited to come back. I was in 2nd grade with Miss Senseney. We moved to a trailer on our same property because my house had mud inside. When I returned to my home, the first thing I saw was my swing. There was trash everywhere. We are fixing our house up now. I am glad to be home!

JASON ORTIZ

"I hope I live here until I'm big!"

When I got home from school, my mom told me that a hurricane was coming so I had to go get my clothes and most of all my shoes. We left our home to go to Dallas. There was a big line. I was so bored and hungry waiting for the line to move. The line finally moved when we were close to Dallas. In about one hour we finally got there. That day, we went to my dad's friend's house. The lady let us borrow her aunt's house. We slept there for three or four days, but the TV antenna didn't work so my other Aunt had a laptop and we watched the news about damage from IKE. We saw a man in Bolivar where I lived and there was a truck in the water probably with people in it. When we came back to be close to home, we stayed in Beaumont with my Aunt and I went to school at Regina Howell. We stayed in Beaumont for about 8 months or less. In December it snowed and I made snow angels. I also made a little snow man with my little cousin. We even had a snowball fight! That night, we ate BBQ. The next day, all the snow was gone except for a little bit. I came back as soon as possible to Bolivar. I saw a lot of cars thrown on people's private property and other places. I felt sad when I arrived where I lived and I saw my house. It was still there and I was so happy. I noticed my garage was messed up. I had left my bike there and I think when it flooded, the salt water made my bike not work. We went to see my Grandma's trailer and it was all gone, not even one thing was there except some of my uncles CD's, some video games and movies. Most places were stinky!

I am happy to be back in Bolivar. Now, I go to school at Crenshaw Elementary and I am very happy here. I wish there was a McDonald's here. This is my favorite Peninsula and I hope I live here until I'm big.

ZACHARY MUNSCH

"I am looking forward to a great year!"

On September 10, 2008, I left Crenshaw School. When I got home, I started boxing my things. I got Star Wars I and III without thinking about Star Wars II or my arrowhead. Then I got my light saber toy, my Star Wars cards, my books and star pilot. I felt OK and scared at the same time.

My family went to my Aunt Susie's house in Baytown. I went to school at High Island. We were back on the Peninsula soon as possible. When we returned, I was devastated. OH NO! Our house was stinky, there was lots of mud and there were a bunch of bibles lying around in the yard.

Now things are getting back to normal, and much better. I am back at Crenshaw. I got new movies like the Alamo, Gettysburg and Sleepy Hollow. Our school, Crenshaw had a talent show at the end of the year and I recited the Gettysburg Address and it goes like this… "Four score and seven years ago, our fathers set forth on this continent a new nation conceived in Liberty and dedicated to the proposition that all men are created equal," and you know the rest.

I would like to see a public library and an observatory in Bolivar. I love to read and love astronomy. I am now living in a camper while my dad is building our home. We should be done with our house by at least Christmas 2009. While building our home, my dad is also building homes for other people on Bolivar Peninsula. I am glad to be back in Bolivar with my dad, mom, sister and brother and looking forward to a great year and moving in my new home.

PAULINA CRUZ

"Bolivar Peninsula is a great place to live!"

When we heard about Hurricane IKE, my mom picked me up from school. We went to our house and got our things. I felt sad because I didn't want to go and it was a long way from our home. We went to Longview to stay with my mom's family, Gomez. I have never met them. When I met them, they were nice to me. I had fun and our families had a nice time visiting. I went to school in Longview.

When we returned to Galveston, I went to Parker Elementary. I didn't like lunchtime at Parker because the food was always cold. I liked the teachers and students, but I missed my friends and Crenshaw School. I was sad when I left Parker. I did not want to go home. I did not want to leave.

When I returned home, I saw a lot of water. The plants were dead because of the saltwater. I lived in a new house because Hurricane IKE took mine down. The storm was so hard on the Peninsula. There were not many houses standing! I didn't feel good because they were falling down. Some houses were still there. I knew that the plants and other things inside my house were gone. My dad built a new house for us to live in. Bolivar Peninsula is a great place to live because we have a beach and some places where people live, do not. I am happy to be back at Crenshaw School! And I would like to say that I am a good person! This is my story. Love, Paulina.

MICHAEL TOVAR

"Bolivar is the best place I have ever lived."

When we heard about Hurricane IKE, my family began putting our things in the car. We went to Austin and lived in cabins. We stayed there for three days.

Next, we moved to a trailer and stayed there for twenty days. Then we moved to Dickinson. We rented a trailer there. I went to school at Hughes Road Elementary. The school was BIG.

I returned to Bolivar. My dad was working on building a new house for us. I attended High Island School because Crenshaw School was not open. When Crenshaw School opened, I was glad. I was in second grade. I had a nice teacher.

I was really glad when my house was ready for us to move in. When I got back home, I was surprised because my house was beautiful. I was glad to be back at Bolivar. It is the best place I have ever lived.

NIVEK SYLVESTRE

"Now, I am happy with what I have."

I was surprised when I came back to Bolivar. I saw a tow truck, a boat, a tree, power lines, a chair, markers, an ATV, a ship, tires, shoes, a desk, trash cans, a clock, glass, windows, anchors, a screen, many books and all kinds of stuff EVERYWHERE! My house was still there, all except my bike which was gone.

At least I have a home. I have a school, the lighthouse, the ferry and some friends. All I have always wanted, although I do miss my little brother, my Aunt Dee and my cousin, J.C. I miss Uncle Jason and my Uncle Pat, (for Patrick), who likes Peterbilts.

Now I am happy with what I have. I have it a little better than in Conroe where I lived before. I am OK with that as long as I have a good heart loving home!!

Bolivar Peninsula Ferry

THE GULF COAST
HURRICANE HISTORY

DATE	STORM NAME	STRENGTH
September 8, 1900	1900 Storm	Category 4
September 11, 1961	Carla	Category 5
August 17, 1969	Camille	Category 5
July 24 & 25, 1979	Claudette	Category 1
August 18, 1983	Alicia	Category 3
August 28, 1992	Andrew	Category 5
June 7 – 9, 2001	Allison	Tropical Storm
September 6, 2004	Francis	Tropical Storm
August 29, 2005	Katrina	Category 3
September 24, 2005	Rita	Category 3
September 12 – 13, 2008	IKE	Category 2

POST IKE:
BOLIVAR PENINSULA, TEXAS TIME LINE

Sept. 10, 2008 – People on the Bolivar Peninsula were ordered to evacuate, despite a projected landfall 100 miles to the south.

Sept. 11, 2008 – Ike made a sudden shift to the north. Forecasters changed IKE's projected path and predicted a direct landfall on Galveston County early Saturday morning as a Category 2 storm. That evening the Galveston-Port Bolivar Ferry ceased operation.

Sept. 12, 2008 – The U.S. Coast Guard and the National Guard air-lifted over 140 people from The Bolivar Peninsula.

Sept. 13, 2008 – IKE made landfall on the Bolivar Peninsula at 2:10 A.M. with 110+ mph winds. President Bush declared Southeast Texas and Southwest Louisiana disaster areas. The media was reporting little about the Peninsula, except that it was gone.

Sept. 14, 2008 – The Bolivar Peninsula is under a "No Fly Zone" warning.

Sept. 15, 2008 –Judge Yarbrough announced a mandatory evacuation of the Bolivar Peninsula. Anyone that stayed during the storm was to now being ordered to leave the peninsula.

Lee Standridge's body was found.

Sept. 16, 2008 – Officials claimed the Bolivar Peninsula had become three separate islands. The State transportation officials said the Bolivar Ferry landing had been badly damaged.

Sept. 18, 2008 – Yarbrough said authorities had completed rescue efforts on Bolivar Peninsula and were turning their focus to recovery.

Sept. 19, 2008 – Bolivar Peninsula residents living east of Rollover Pass were being allowed to return to survey property damage.

Sept. 24, 2008 - The body of Gail Ettenger from Gilchrist was found in the marsh on the mainland.

County Judge Jim Yarbrough said the recovery for Bolivar Peninsula would be "longer than we ever imagined." He said it might take six months just to restore power.

Sept. 25, 2008 – Rescue workers found the body of a woman believed to be from the Bolivar Peninsula in a debris field in Chambers County.

Sept. 26, 2008 – Residents of the Bolivar Peninsula were allowed to return to their home as a "Look and Leave" program. Over 5,000 people safely entered the Peninsula on this day. The look, work and leave program will continue until the Rollover Pass Bridge is again available for two way traffic.

Sept. 28, 2008 – A woman's body approx. 30 – 50 years old was found on Pelican Island.

Oct. 3, 2008 - County Commissioner Pat Doyle emphatically stressed, "I want to make it very clear, and the Galveston County Commissioners are not closing the Peninsula." When the bridge is fixed and both lanes are open, we will look at opening up the Peninsula. Pods are currently being operated at two sites - High Island Football Field Parking Lot and the Joe Faggard Community Center at Crystal Beach. Bolivar Peninsula Special Utility District, (BPSUD), has re-established water service in High Island with a "Boil Water Notice" in effect. Within the next couple of weeks, the BPSUD hopes to have a trunk line to the Port Bolivar area. Entergy Electric is working almost around the clock to provide electric service to the Peninsula. Power will be restored to High Island by the end of this weekend and to the rest of the Peninsula within three (3) months. Debris Removal is an issue that will require patience. However, property owners should push their debris (separated into piles - vegetative, construction demolition, appliances, vehicles and sand) to the edge of the public right-of-way to help speed the process of pick-up. The County is working with FEMA to get approval for Personal Property Debris Removal, (PPDR), and will provide updated information as soon as it is available. The County will need assistance contacting property owners for Right of Entry Documentation. The County contact for PPDR will be Garrett Foskit. Analysis is currently being conducted to determine the category of damages to structures throughout the unincorporated areas of the County and Permits are about one month away. FEMA has indicated that modular housing will be available. County has established a committee and obtaining damage assessments now and mitigation issues thru-out the unincorporated areas.

TxDot, (Texas Department of Transportation), has said that the Ferry landing has to be dredged to get up and running again and that it will take approximately 6 weeks before multiple Ferrys are up and running. Two boats will be running in six weeks and in two months two landings will be repaired and back to regular service. No residential, business employees or pedestrian traffic will be allowed at this time. It will take approximately 6 weeks before the public will be able to use the Ferry. This is purely a safety issue.

TxDot will begin repairs to Rollover Pass and should be completed within 45 days. Check Point at Rollover Pass will remain until the 45 day period is up or the repairs are completed. After repairs are completed we hope to open the Peninsula with adequate security.

The Corps of Engineers is going to begin with the dredging in the Inter Coastal Waterway from Port Bolivar to High Island, including the Rollover Bay and Ferry Landing. Dredging will result in replenishing our beaches. This should resort in 1.5 million cubic yards of sand.

Building Permits will begin to be issued in 5-6 weeks. If a home is missing stairs and minor repairs need to be made to the structure, those repairs can be made without a permit. However, once everything is inspected modifications to existing properties may need to be made to bring structure up to code.

The curfew, to clarify the program is set for 6:00 A.M. to 2:00 P.M. for entry on to the Bolivar Peninsula; begin leaving at 4:00 P.M. and off the Peninsula by 6:00 P.M. Bolivar is still under the vacate and curfew order west of Rollover Pass. NO EXCEPTIONS! Property owners can also send contractors on their behalf with proper documentation, which is a letter authorizing and proof of residence they are going to work on.

Oct. 4, 2008 – An elderly woman under 5'2" was found on Goat Island.

Oct. 5, 2008 – The Tiki Bar & Grill and Coconuts are serving free meals via generator until electricity is restored. Seaside Lumber and Parker Lumber are open and operating with the bare essentials.

Oct. 6, 2008 - A burn ban has been issued for all of the Bolivar Peninsula.

Rollover Pass Bridge will not be shut down for any extended length of time. Forty-five days from today, the bridge should be completely repaired.

During the "look and leave" visiting the Bolivar Peninsula - Be sure to take several cans of Fix-A-Flat with you when you go, along with your driver's license, proof of ownership (deed, water or utility bill.) Per Constable William Comeaux, there are still Porta-Potties in different locations up and down the Peninsula and several at City Hall. You should plan to bring your own food and water.

A white male under 5'10" was found on Goat Island.

Oct. 7, 2008 - SCR Construction Co., Inc. was awarded the Rollover Bridge project in the amount of $643,381.50. There is currently 1 lane; work is to repair/replace the entire bridge. It is a 45 day project and the projection for completion is November 26, 2008. The goal is to have 2 lanes open before or by Thanksgiving. Intermittently for 10 minutes to switch traffic, etc. No scheduled or lengthy closure dates are set. Work will be 7 days a week, beginning at sun up and ending at sunset.

If the roads are cleared and passable the earliest that Peninsula inspections could start is October 27, 2008 and the earliest permits could be issued for non GLO, (General Land Office), and non Health District locations will be around November 20, 2008. Remember most of Peninsula permits will be Health District related because unlike the mainland there is no public sewer system there. Permits within 1000 feet of the beach will be GLO related.

Oct. 8, 2008 –For more security, there are 4 single-man police units on days, 4 single-man units on nights. The same shifts being manned on the weekends.

We want to encourage folks to make sure their property is secured removing items that don't need to be there, particularly of the structure is damaged.

INSPECTIONS IN UNINCORPORATED AREAS:

High Island	100%
Gilchrist	0%
Caplen	0%
Crystal Beach	80%

In Crystal Beach the sand is pushed to the side, clearing down to the pavement. In some places the road may only be as wide as one lane, but it is clear to the asphalt. The 80% is from Los Patos to Jack's Road (near the Outrigger or Coconuts restaurants).

Bolivar	90%

All of Bolivar on the Bay side is complete. There is work to be completed near the north jetty and around the Magnolia Area.

- It is estimated 4-6 working days to complete Crystal Beach and Bolivar.

The "official" email from connects at TxDOT. They are working with USCG, (United States Coast Guard), to draw new soundings of Bolivar Roads, attempting to find a new pathway. Ferry may be out only until Monday providing those folks are able to find the new "roadway." If that doesn't work, they'll be out until the dredge gets there, which is at least a month away. This will likely hamper cleanup, fire services accessing the Peninsula from Galveston, etc.

The Health District will require that all persons needing a building permit, from Engineering, to make repairs, will have to contract with a certified septic system installers to review the condition of the existing septic system.

Oct. 10, 2008 - Eligibility and timing for a manufactured housing unit - either at a FEMA-developed trailer park or a citizen's own lot - is the same. Individuals who register with FEMA go through a PPI (Pre-Placement Interview), much of which can be conducted at a DRC. There is a DRC located in High Island. It is during this PPI process that FEMA determines whether an individual is best suited for rental assistance (apartment, hotel), a mobile home park (typically for people who were renting before the storm) or a modular home on their property. Rental assistance is typically for 18 months, whether it's for a hotel or use of a FEMA trailer.

Key point is that individuals must get through that DRC, which is why there should be more DRC's open on the mainland. Mobile registration trailers in High Island and Jamaica Beach are being converted to full mobile DRC's, which can take care of that all-important PPI. One of these mobiles could then be relocated down the line to West County Bldg. or other needed location. Some modular housing will need to be located in the 100-year floodplain. FEMA requires the county to sign a letter permitting FEMA to park trailers in the floodplain. This letter is on the agenda for 10-15-08.

Everyone who is a registered voter is eligible to vote.

The voting location is: St. Mathews United Methodist Church,
1308 Weeks Avenue, High Island

Oct. 12, 2008 – Many of our churches have started having Sunday Worship Services in tents or in their parking lots.

Oct. 20, 2008 - Extended hours for the curfew are now from 6:00 PM - 6:00 AM.

Early Voting Dates and Times
Monday, Oct. 20th - Saturday, Oct. 25th 7:00 AM - 7:00 PM
Sunday, Oct. 26th 1:00 PM - 6:00 PM
Monday, Oct. 27th - Friday, Oct. 31st 7:00 AM - 7:00 PM

County roads that need to be temporarily repaired are being assessed as soon as possible. TxDOT and County Right of Way's is in Phase I, which is to collect sand and debris. Currently all of Galveston's County's Road and Bridge crew and equipment are dedicated to restoring the roads on Bolivar Peninsula.

Debris removal will begin by the end of this week or early next week. We will be providing debris collection status reports as we move forward.

Oct. 23, 2008 - TxDot and County Right of Way's Phase I is 99% complete.

Oct. 25, 2008 – An older white male was found on a jetty near Port Bolivar.

Oct. 30, 2008 - The debris removal contract has been awarded to Crowder Gulf. Removal of debris should begin Friday, October 31, and we should see good progress immediately. Crowder Gulf will have 80 trucks removing right of way debris and sand. Commercial properties are not included under the PPDR; they must remove debris and place in Right of Way.

Search and recovery will continue ongoing efforts to search all debris piles on Bolivar Peninsula and Goat Island.

A representative from the Engineers office will be on the Peninsula at Crystal Beach on Saturday, November 1, 2008 and on Sunday, November 2, 2008 from 8 AM - 5PM at 1987 Matt St., behind the Crystal Beach Post Office. They will be there to hand out and assist in filling out forms.

FEMA has granted Galveston County PPDR (Private Property Debris Removal), program. This program allows the County to enter onto private property to remove certain types of debris and still qualify for FEMA reimbursements. It pertains to private residences only. NOTE: Demolition of Private structures and removal by county is not allowed at this time, but will be reviewed on a case by case basis. Commercial properties are not included under the PPDR - must remove debris and place in Right-of-way.

After meeting with FEMA we are looking to develop multiple community sites on Bolivar Peninsula. We are not sure of the time frame yet, but are moving forward on the detailed analysis of creating the sites. We also confirmed that the motel/ hotel arrangements have been extended to January 15, 2009, and the daily rate has been increased to $160.00.

POWER –
CATEGORY 1 - Structures, (no damage), we have released power.
CATEGORY 2 - Structures, (non-substantially damaged), power only will be released after health district has notified the County
Engineer's office via fax and the County Engineer's office have issued a repair permit.

CATEGORY 3 - Structures, (substantially damaged), power only will be released after the health district has notified the County

Engineer's office via fax and the County Engineer's office have issued a permit to repair to the proper elevation.

Nov. 4, 2008 – Body found in Chambers County.

Nov. 5, 2008 - The Rollover Pass Bridge will be closed from Wednesday 6:00 P.M. - Thursday, 6:00 A.M. For those who do not want to stay on the Peninsula should make plans to be on the High Island side of the Rollover Pass Bridge prior to 6 PM. The bridge closing is necessary to facilitate the installation of the new waterline on the north side of the bridge.

Boats have been removed off the causeway and from IH-45, FM 646, FM 517 (San Leon) area and FM 3005. Debris crews everywhere with concentration on 3005 and service road IH-45 and throughout the county roadways. Beginning Monday, November 10, 2008, Galveston County will remove the vacate order. The new curfew will still be in effect from 10 PM - 6 AM. Search and recovery will continue ongoing efforts to search all debris piles on Bolivar Peninsula and on Goat Island.

Crowder Gulf has been removing debris since Friday, October 31, 2008, and progress is coming along.

Nov. 6, 2008- Effective Monday
- No vacate order - residents can stay
- Opening up at Checkpoint.
- If you have not secured your personal property or belongings by now, please do so immediately.
- Galveston County Sheriff Office and Constable's office will also increase the number of units beginning next week.
- Hopefully Ferry services restored shortly.

Nov. 7, 2008 - Please be advised to use caution in traveling the Bolivar Peninsula. Many of the beach-front roads are washed out and have drop offs; and washed out roads along Hwy 87 have been temporarily repaired only. Our debris removal company has a large number of trucks commuting back and forth from the county ROW's to their Temp Debris Removal Sites along the Peninsula. Traffic signals are inoperable and have been replaced temporarily with 4 way stops at all main intersections. Please use extreme caution.

SAND - PLEASE DO NOT REMOVE SAND FROM THE COUNTY OR STATE RIGHT OF WAY (ROW), IT IS AGAINST THE LAW UNDER EITHER SCENARIO AND IT IS BEING ENFORCED.

Nov. 10, 2008 - The North landing of the Ferry is open and it has been tested. Ferry service will be open to the Public at 6:00 A.M. on Tuesday, November 11th.

Nov. 11, 2008 – The Ferry is open to the Public.

Nov. 12, 2008 - The Galveston County Debris Hotline number has been issued. The Galveston County Sheriff's Office has said that more Department of Public Safety troopers will be patrolling the Peninsula, along with more Galveston County Sheriff's Officers and the Constable's presence is there as always. This should help security on the Peninsula.

The POD will be open thru the weekend and closing it down after that. Services to the Peninsula are opening up. Supplies should begin to be readily available.

Nov. 19, 2008 – The Crystal Beach Medical Clinic re-opened in a new location at 955 East Road.

Nov. 25, 2008 - The debris contractors are on a break for the holidays. It will be faster if the homeowners can move the debris out to the ROW rather than go through the PPDR. All Right of Entry inquiries need to be directed to the Galveston County Debris information trailer located behind the County Annex in Crystal Beach.

Deadline for SBA submission is December 12, 2008. Small Business Administration, (SBA), Disaster Loan Outreach Center will be open at the High Island School, Mon. - Fri. From 9 AM - 5 PM until further notice. They can help you with your loan application and answer other questions. No appointment is necessary.

Jennifer McLemore's body found 12 miles from her home in Gilchrist.

Nov. 26, 2008 - All emergency repairs are complete and two-way traffic has been restored on the Rollover Pass Bridge.

Dec. 10, 2008 – Only 46% of residents who received disaster housing vouchers had found a place to rent.

A badly decomposed body was found in a debris pile on Goat Island.

Jan. 2009 – Swede's Quick Stop re-opened.

Residents who relied on waivers to qualify for windstorm insurance were warned they would lose coverage if repairs didn't meet the new codes.

Feb. 4, 2009 – Crenshaw Elementary re-opened.

Feb. 2009 – Stingaree Restaurant and La Playita are now open.

Feb. 15, 2009 – The Big Store (formally Gulf Coast Market) re-opened part of the store.

Feb. 21, 2009 – The biggest Bolivar Peninsula Mardi Gras ever!

Feb. 2009 – The search for bodies on the Bolivar Peninsula ended.

A Crystal beach house that survived IKE accidentally was demolished by a contractor. The Crystal Beach Post Office re-opened.

Mar. 15, 2009 – The Latitude 29.2 Surf Shop re-opened part of the store.

Mar. 21, 2009 – The T.J.'s Convenience Store re-opened.

May 29 – 31, 2009 – The Stingaree Music Festival and the Crab Festival joined together and put on the festival.

Mar. 2009 – A contractor removing storm debris in Port Bolivar found a casket with a man's body inside. The body was returned to its grave in a few days.

More than 750 people, 90% from Bolivar Peninsula applied for government buyouts for their IKE damaged properties.

The county created a steering committee to map out a long-term recovery plan for the Bolivar Peninsula.

About ½ of the elderly residents have not returned.

Birds are starting to reappear on the Peninsula! Bill Reid built a new liquor store and renamed it, Lite House Liquor Store. Many of the telephone land lines are starting to work.

Apr. 15, 2009 – Former President George H. Bush and Former Secretary of State, James Baker III visited the Bolivar Peninsula for beach cleanup.

Apr. 2009 – Dannay's Doughnut Shop built a new store and opened up. Many other businesses have started opening up, including Pat's Tire, Tropical Accents Coastal Décor and Fun & Sun Beachwear Shop

May 2009 – IKE was retired as a storm name.

Property owners trying to make general repairs are waiting as long as 6 weeks for Building permits.

June 2009 – Parishioners got a temporary restraining order barring the Archdiocese of Galveston-Houston from demolishing Our Mother of Mercy Catholic Church. Bolivar churchgoers protested outside a Mass celebrated by Cardinal Daniel Dinardo in regards to this demolition.

Aug. 29, 2009 – the 4th Annual Endless Summer Bash.

Sept. 13, 2009 – The Hurricane IKE 1 Year Anniversary Memorial Service and Celebration was held at the Crenshaw Elementary School.